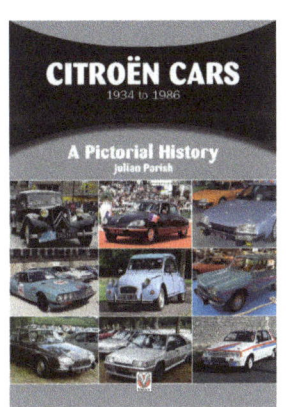

Other titles in the Pictorial History series
BMW Cars 1945 to 2013 (Alder)
Austin Cars 1948 to 1990 (Rowe)
Ford Cars – Ford UK cars 1945-1995 (Rowe)
Jaguar Cars 1946 to 2008 (Thorley)
Lotus Cars 1952 to 2024 (Parish)
Morris Cars 1948-1984 (Newell)
Riley & Wolseley Cars of the 1950s, 1960s and 1970s (Rowe)
Rootes Cars of the 50s, 60s & 70s – Hillman, Humber, Singer, Sunbeam & Talbot (Rowe)
Rover Cars 1945 to 2005 (Taylor)
Triumph & Standard Cars 1945 to 1984 (Warrington)
Vauxhall Cars 1945 to 1995 (Alder)

www.veloce.co.uk

First published in August 2022, reprinted June 2023 and 2025 by Veloce, an imprint of David and Charles Limited. Tel +44 (0)1305 260068 / e-mail info@veloce.co.uk / web www.veloce.co.uk.
ISBN: 978-1-787116-36-8
© 2022, 2023& 2025 Julian Parish and David and Charles. All rights reserved. With the exception of quoting brief passages for the purpose of review, no part of this publication may be recorded, reproduced or transmitted by any means, including photocopying, without the written permission of David and Charles Limited.
Throughout this book logos, model names and designations, etc, have been used for the purposes of identification, illustration and decoration. Such names are the property of the trademark holder as this is not an official publication. Readers with ideas for automotive books, or books on other transport or related hobby subjects, are invited to write to the editorial director of Veloce at the above email address. British Library Cataloguing in Publication Data – A catalogue record for this book is available from the British Library. Design and DTP by Veloce.

CITROËN CARS
1934 to 1986

A Pictorial History
Julian Parish

CONTENTS

Citroën: a brief introduction 5

Acknowledgements 8

Traction Avant 9

DS and ID 26

CX 48

SM 62

2CV and derivatives 72

Ami and M35 97

GS and GSA 108

BX 124

Other models from the 1970s and 1980s 134

Index 152

(For full model listing see the Index)

Citroën: a brief introduction

Born in Paris in 1878, André Citroën first made his mark as chairman of the car manufacturer Mors from 1908-1914. During World War I he set up and ran a major arms factory at the Quai de Javel in Paris, and in 1919 he founded his own company, Automobiles Citroën, using the former arms factory to build his cars. Its first Type A models went on sale the same year.

André Citroën had a clear vision of the need for affordable, mass-produced cars, following the example of the Ford Model T. During the 1920s, Citroën's models were relatively conventional in design, but were well engineered and soon established a reputation for their solid build. The success of Citroën's half-tracked vehicles in the 'Croisière noire' and 'Croisière jaune' long-distance expeditions reinforced this image, as did the endurance records set by 'La Petite Rosalie' at Montlhéry in 1932.

This story opens in 1934, when the revolutionary new Traction Avant (or front-wheel drive) model was unveiled. The range

'La Petite Rosalie' returns to Montlhéry.

expanded to include four- and six-light saloons, cabriolets, and fixed-head coupés. They were the first in a long line of cars which would become famous throughout the world for their technical innovation, distinctive styling and unrivalled comfort.

The introduction of the Traction Avant took its toll, however, both on the business and on the health of its founder. The cost of developing the new model and rebuilding the factory for it, as well as Citroën's imaginative

C4G saloon from 1932, on show at Epoqu'Auto in Lyon.

Citroën Cars 1934 to 1986 – A Pictorial History

On Citroën's test track at La Ferté-Vidame. (Courtesy Citroën Communication)

but expensive marketing campaigns, drained the company's finances, and by the end of 1934 Automobiles Citroën was forced to file for bankruptcy. It was taken over by the tyre company Michelin, its main creditor, and André Citroën died of cancer the following year.

Citroën caused another sensation when it launched the 2CV in 1948, bringing affordable motoring to postwar France. Always powered by the inimitable air-cooled flat-twin, the 2CV gradually became more powerful and equipment slightly less spartan. The company developed light vans and the Dyane and Méhari models on the same platform, but the original 2CV outlasted them all.

The Traction Avant made way for the radical new DS in 1955. This again created a stir when it was launched, with its futuristic styling and extensive use of hydraulic systems for its suspension, steering, brakes and gear change. Over its 20-year career, its engines became

Late 1950s 2CV. (Courtesy Citroën Communication)

Citroën: a brief introduction

The DS, like this DS 23 Pallas seen in Caen, always pleases the crowds.

progressively larger and more powerful, while a simpler ID model was introduced alongside it. As well as the four-door saloons and spacious estates, the DS was also available as an elegant convertible.

The DS was, in turn, replaced from 1974 by the CX. Arguably less of a surprise than the DS or Traction Avant, it was nonetheless acclaimed for its modern styling, interior space and improved visibility. The saloon and estate versions of the CX enjoyed a long career through the 1970s and 1980s.

Each of these models is presented in detail, together with the exclusive Maserati-engined SM coupé, unveiled in 1970, and the models that were introduced to fill the gap between the basic 2CV and Citroën's large saloons: the Ami and later the GS and GSA. The cars built at Slough in the UK, where Citroën had a factory from 1926-1966, are also included.

By 1974 and the time of the oil crisis, however, the company faced new challenges, and once again struggled to absorb high product development costs and investments in its factories. Peugeot, until then one of its major rivals, had to step in to save it from bankruptcy. In 1976, Peugeot increased its stake to 90% and the PSA Group was formed.

CX 25 Prestige on show at Rétromobile in Paris.

The SM celebrated its 50th anniversary in 2020.

*BX 16 RS.
(Courtesy Citroën Communication/ Georges Guyot)*

Over the next decade, some of Citroën's innovative spirit lived on in models such as the GSA, BX and the Romanian-built Axel. Gradually, however, the need to spread costs across the PSA Group led to greater uniformity and more conventional designs, as can be seen in cars such as the LN and Visa.

During the 1990s and 2000s, Citroën's XM and C6 flagships continued to use the company's famed hydropneumatic suspension, but many of its other cars seemed increasingly ordinary. The DS name returned in 2009, before being spun off as a stand-alone premium marque in 2015. Only recently have Citroëns like the C4 Cactus or the electric Ami runabout, launched in 2020, rediscovered some of the distinctive character that was the hallmark of the company's cars during the 20th century.

Acknowledgements

Several organisations and individuals have generously allowed me to reproduce their photographs in this book, and it is my pleasure to thank John Handcock of Citroën UK, Henri Fradet of the Citromuseum, Lynnie Farrant at Bonhams, Sandrine Fargeix at Michelin, Iris Hummel from Artcurial, and Baptiste Nicolosi from Osenat, as well as Paul Buckett, Jeremy Clarke and Chris Hughes. In France, the Conservatoire Citroën was a valuable source of information, as were the many books and articles by the late Thierry Astier. Every English-speaking Citroën enthusiast owes a huge debt of gratitude to Julian Marsh, who has built up the remarkable Citroënët website. Finally, my thanks are due once again to Rod Grainger, Becky Martin and the team at Veloce Publishing.

*The new Ami.
(Courtesy Citroën Communication)*

Traction Avant

Citroën did not invent front-wheel drive, but it was the first manufacturer to put it into mass production. Developed under the direction of André Lefèbvre, originally an aeronautical engineer, the Traction Avant was launched in the spring of 1934. It marked a huge step forward for Citroën and for automotive design as a whole. As well as front-wheel drive, it had an advanced suspension design using torsion bars, which was fully independent at the front and semi-independent at the rear. It was also one of the first to adopt rack and pinion steering in 1936.

The Traction Avant was the first mass-produced car with a monocoque construction rather than a separate chassis and body. This met with considerable scepticism at first, but Citroën successfully demonstrated its superior crash resistance. The model's styling was the work of Flaminio Bertoni, a young Italian designer and sculptor, and its body was much lower and more aerodynamic than Citroën's previous square-cut saloons. All the cars had rear-hinged front doors and, where fitted, conventional rear doors.

The Traction Avant was primarily conceived as a four-seat saloon, with a 7CV French fiscal horsepower rating, and priced at no more than 15,000FF. The design brief for the car targeted a kerb weight of 800kg (1764lb), a 100km/h (62mph) top speed, and an average fuel consumption of 7 litres per 100km (40mpg). It had a new engine designed by Maurice Sainturat, an overhead-valve unit with three main bearings, and removable piston liners. Cooling was taken care of by a water pump, thermostat and fan. It was originally intended that the engine would be mated to a Sensaud de Lavaud automatic gearbox, but

Production line for the Traction Avant. (Courtesy Citroën Communication)

the high cost of developing this led to it being dropped shortly before the car's launch, and all production cars had a three-speed manual gearbox with a distinctive 'cow's tail' gearlever protruding from the dashboard. During the model's long career from 1934-1957, several different engine sizes were produced or planned.

The Traction Avant was available in a variety of different body styles. The four-light saloons accounted for the majority of production and are sometimes referred to as the 'Berline Légère' (light saloon) or, with a longer wheelbase, the 'Berline Normale' (normal saloon). Longer still, the nine-seat Familiale, Limousine and Commerciale models had a six-light body, the last of them featuring a hatchback. Alongside these models, the stylish Cabriolet was a two-seat roadster with an additional folding dickey seat, while the 'Faux Cabriolet' was an elegant fixed-head coupé. Both these versions were produced only before the Second World War.

The war brought production of Citroën's cars to a virtual standstill, so the Traction Avant's career is most easily seen in two phases: before and after the conflict. It was certainly not forgotten during this time though, when it was famously used by the French Resistance.

The Traction Avant was no sports car, but its durability and handling nonetheless ensured it won a number of events in competition.

Familiale. (Courtesy Citroën Communication)

In 1949, Gaston Gautruche won the Coupe des Alpes (the Alpine Rally) driving an 11BL; from 1950-1952, Citroën won the Lyon-Charbonnières Rally three years in a row,

Duotone paintwork sets off the lines of this Cabriolet.

twice with an 11CV and once with a 15CV. It also competed in period in the Monte-Carlo Rally and Tour de France Automobile, so guaranteeing it the right to enter the revival versions of both events today.

Altogether, 759,123 Traction Avants were built, well over 90% of them with four-cylinder engines. This total included 26,400 cars assembled in England, 31,750 at Forest near Brussels in Belgium, 1823 at Cologne in Germany, and 550 at Copenhagen in Denmark. The model enjoys a tremendous following to this day, with the support of numerous international clubs and specialist publications.

At Citroën's Centenary Celebration at La Ferté-Vidame in 2019.

7CV

Original 1934 7CV at Rétromobile, Paris in 2019. (Courtesy Citroën Communication)

Citroën began production of the Traction Avant on 19 April 1934, after presenting it to its dealers at the end of March. The first version was the 7A, but this was probably put into production too early, as its 1.3-litre engine was immediately considered underpowered and it was soon uprated. In any event, the 7A was built for only three months, making it highly sought after by collectors today. It was available only as a four-door saloon and had a fabric roof and a single windscreen wiper.

In July 1934, the 7A was replaced by the 7B, which had a larger 1.5-litre engine (actually taking it into the French 9CV tax class), an all-

11

Citroën Cars 1934 to 1986 – A Pictorial History

Concours d'élégance for 7CVs at the Bois de Boulogne near Paris. (Courtesy Citroën Communication)

steel roof and twin windscreen wipers. The 7B also became available as an elegant Cabriolet and Faux Cabriolet. Alongside the 7B, Citroën introduced the 7 Sport, with a 1.9-litre engine (making it technically an 11CV model).

The 7B's career was equally short-lived: in 1935, it made way for the 7C, with a further increase in engine capacity and power output. The 7 Sport meanwhile was replaced by the 11 Légère. Telescopic dampers replaced the friction dampers fitted to the 7A and 7B. In 1936, the luggage compartment could be opened from outside the car, and the radiator grille was painted rather than chrome-plated. In May that year, all Traction Avant models gained rack and pinion steering, followed in 1937 by Michelin 'Pilote' wheels and wider wings. The final changes to the 7C came in 1939, when it became the 7C Economique, with a different carburettor delivering 10% lower fuel consumption. Production of the 7CV came to an end in 1941 and did not resume after the war.

François Lecot, a restaurateur from Rochetaillée-sur-Saône, near Lyon, was an early convert to the virtues of Citroën's new model, driving virtually non-stop from Paris to Moscow and back in October 1934. He would be back behind the wheel of an 11CV the following year for another adventure …

NUMBER PRODUCED: All 7CV models 1934-1941: 88,066, including 7A: 7000; 7B: 15,620. Years built: 1934-1941.
PRICES: (July 1934) saloon: 17,700FF; Cabriolet: 18,700FF; Faux Cabriolet: 18,700FF.
ENGINE: Water-cooled, four-cylinder petrol, longitudinally mounted with gearbox at front, OHV layout. 7A: Bore 72mm, stroke 80mm, capacity 1303cc, maximum power 32bhp at 3200rpm; 7B: Bore 78mm, stroke 80mm, capacity 1529cc, maximum power 35bhp at 3200rpm; 7C: Bore 72mm, stroke

1934 Faux Cabriolet. (Courtesy Citroën Communication)

Traction Avant

The boot could only be accessed from inside the car on the first models built. (Courtesy Citroën Communication)

100mm, capacity 1628cc, maximum power 36bhp at 3800rpm; Solex downdraught carburettor on all versions.
TRANSMISSION: Front-wheel drive, three-speed manual gearbox with synchromesh on second and third, dashboard-mounted selector.
BRAKES: Drums at front and rear, hydraulically operated.
TYRES: 140 X 40 (Michelin).
SUSPENSION: Front: independent, using longitudinal torsion bars and wishbone set-up; rear: beam axle with Panhard rod, trailing arms and transverse torsion bars. 7A and 7B: friction dampers; 7C: telescopic dampers.
STEERING: Gemmer-type worm and roller until 05/1936, then rack and pinion.
DIMENSIONS: Length: 4.35m (171.3in); width: 1.56m (61.4in); height: 1.52m (59.8in); wheelbase: 2.91m (114.6in); turning circle: 11m (36ft).
KERB WEIGHT: 900kg (1984lb).
CAPACITIES: Fuel: 45l (9.9gal); boot: 0.13m^3 (4.6ft^3).
COLOURS (1934): Noir, Rouge Bordeaux, Gris Perle, Bleu Marine, Beige Rosé and Beige Maintenon for main bodywork, with black wings and black wheels.

Rat look, anyone? Some 7CVs, like this one from 1938, have still to be restored.

François Lecot at the end of his drive from Paris to Moscow and back in 1934. (Courtesy Citroën Communication)

11CV

The 11CV was presented at the end of 1934. It was longer and wider than the 7CV models, which continued in production. This time, its name correctly indicated that it was rated at 11CV in France, and it used the 1911cc engine (now with 'Pausodyne' mounts) which would remain a staple of Citroën's engine production until the first years of the DS and ID.

The 11CV's bigger engine gave the car much improved performance, with no better demonstration than the endurance record set by François Lecot in 1935-1936. He covered 400,000km (nearly 250,000 miles), driving every day for a year between Paris, Lyon and Monte-Carlo.

The 11CV was available from launch as a five/six-seat saloon, roadster (Cabriolet) with a folding hood and fold-down windscreen, and as a fixed-head coupé (Faux Cabriolet). The term 'Large' on Cabriolet models indicates the wider body and track. Customers could also choose a long-wheelbase, six-light version in saloon, five/six-seat Limousine and Familiale form. The last of these had an additional row of folding seats in the rear compartment, making it possible for the driver to carry eight passengers. A long-wheelbase taxi was also offered, with a screen between the driver and passengers.

Like the 7CV, in 1936 the 11CV gained an external boot opening and a painted radiator grille, as well as rack and pinion steering. In 1937, the 11 was renamed the 11B, while the 11 Légère (11AL) became the 11BL. The speedometer and other instruments were redesigned and repositioned in front of the driver, and both models were now equipped with Michelin 'Pilote' wheels. Three iridescent finishes (a kind of coarse metallic) were added to the range of colours.

Finally, in 1939, the four-door saloon version of the 11CV gained an extra 10bhp and the suffix 'Performance' was added to its name. 1939 also saw the launch of the Commerciale

version, using the long-wheelbase six-light body, but with fold-down rear seats and a two-piece tailgate. The lower part of the tailgate could be opened to form a platform for ease of loading or to carry longer items, while the upper part was hinged at the roof. Citroën promoted the Commerciale as a dual-purpose vehicle which could be used as a van with a 500kg (1102lb) payload during the week and as a five-seat family car at the weekend. By 1939, however, both the Cabriolet and Faux Cabriolet had gone out of production.

After the war, production of the Traction Avant slowly got under way again. The 7CV had been dropped, so the range began with the 11CV saloons, available as the 11 Légère

Early 11CV saloon from 1934: note the pair of lateral vents.

1938 11B Cabriolet delights the crowd at a concours d'élégance at Deauville.

Left: period advertisement for 1938 11B Cabriolet. Right: interior of 1938 11B Cabriolet. (Both courtesy Citroën Communication/Georges Guyot)

Citroën Cars 1934 to 1986 – A Pictorial History

The styling of the Faux Cabriolet resembled the open model, but with a fixed roof.

Spacious rear bench on six-light Familiale and Limousine. (Courtesy Citroën Communication)

and 11 Normale, the latter having the longer wheelbase and wider track. These postwar models can be recognised by the series of louvres to each side of the engine that had previously been reserved for the 15 Six, rather than a pair of opening vents. Plain steel wheels with small chrome hubcaps were now fitted, while the headlamp surrounds were painted rather than chrome-plated.

The 11 Normale gained a new radiator

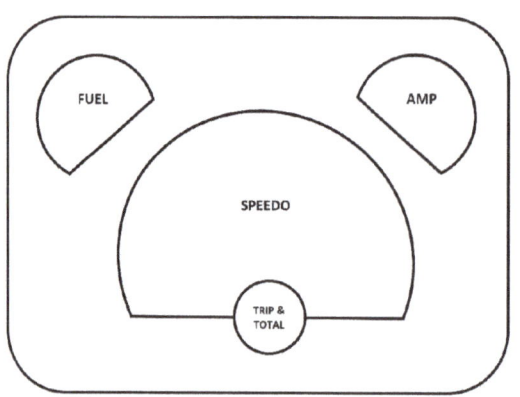

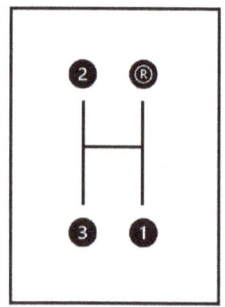

Dashboard and gear change layout of the 11CV.

16

Traction Avant

grille in 1949 and – together with the other 11CV models – another 2bhp in 1950. Inside the car, from July 1949 the dashboard instruments had a white rather than black background, but kept the same layout. In 1953, an extended boot was fitted, almost doubling its capacity, and the Familiale went back on sale. It was followed in 1954 by the Commerciale, which now had a single-piece tailgate. As shown in the data below, a wider range of colours was available for the final years of 11CV production, from 1954-1957.

As the DS was launched in 1955 and the Traction Avant prepared to bow out, the 11D Légère and 11D Normale were fitted with a revised 11D engine developing 60bhp. This would be carried over into the DS 19 at its launch in 1955. Production of all Traction Avant models finally came to an end in France and at Forest in Belgium in 1957, when the cheaper and less complex ID 19 was introduced alongside the DS.

NUMBER PRODUCED: 571,995 (in France); years built: 1934-1957.
ENGINE: Water-cooled, four-cylinder petrol, longitudinally mounted with gearbox at front, OHV layout. Bore 78mm, stroke 100mm, capacity 1911cc, maximum power 56bhp at 3800rpm, Solex 32 BPIC downdraught carburettor.
TRANSMISSION: Front-wheel drive, three-speed manual gearbox with synchromesh on second and third, dashboard-mounted selector. Final drive ratio: 3.44:1; gear ratios first 3.80:1; second 2.12:1; third 1.25:1.

Commerciale models from 1939 and 1954, with different tailgate arrangements.

Postwar 11CV saloon: note side louvres. This car has numerous chrome accessories.

17

Citroën Cars 1934 to 1986 – A Pictorial History

Enlarged boot fitted (at last!) from 1953 to standard saloons, as well as to Familiale models like this. (Courtesy Citroën Communication)/ Godbert)

Proof that not all Traction Avants were black ...

Iceland Blue (Bleu d'Islande).

Heather Grey (Gris Bruyère).

Last 11CV off the line. (Courtesy Citroën Communication)

BRAKES: drums at front and rear, hydraulically operated.
TYRES: 165 X 400 (Michelin); Familiale 185 X 400 (Michelin).
SUSPENSION: Front: independent, using longitudinal torsion bars and wishbone set-up; rear: beam axle with Panhard rod, trailing arms and transverse torsion bars; telescopic dampers.

Night Blue (Bleu de Nuit).

15 Six

STEERING: Rack and pinion.
DIMENSIONS: Normale: Length: 4.62m (181.9in); width: 1.71m (67.3in); height: 1.54m (60.6in); wheelbase: 3.09m (121.7in). Familiale (where different): Length: 4.80m (189.0in); wheelbase: 3.27m (128.8in).
KERB WEIGHT: Normale 1000kg (2205lb); Familiale 1070kg (2359lb).
CAPACITIES: Fuel: 50l (11.0gal); boot: 0.13m^3 (4.6ft^3), from 1953: 0.23m^3 (8.1ft^3).
COLOURS
1934-1941: Noir, Rouge Bordeaux, Gris Perle, Bleu Marine, Beige Rosé and Beige Maintenon for main bodywork, with black or matching wings and wheels depending on year, Beige Irisé, Gris Irisé and Bleu Irisé from 1937, Vert Irisé on Familiale and Vert Olive on Cabriolet from 1938.
1945-1947: Body and wings: Vert Armée, Gris Clair Irisé, Gris Foncé Irisé, Noir, with grey or ivory wheels.
1948-1953: Black (Noir) only, with ivory wheels.
1953-1954: Body and wings: Noir, Bleu RAF, Gris Perle and Bleu d'Islande, with colour of wheels depending on body colour.
1954-1957: Body and wings: Noir, Gris Perle, Bleu de Nuit and Gris Bruyère, with colour of wheels depending on body colour.

The 15 Six was introduced in June 1938 after Citroën had to abort its plans to offer an eight-cylinder model, the 22CV, at the top of the Traction Avant range. Despite its name, it was technically a 16CV model in France from the start. It shared its main bodyshell and wheelbase with the 11B, but the bonnet was lengthened to house the new six-cylinder engine. Full-scale production only began in 1939, so few cars were built before the war brought the assembly lines to a halt. Citroën planned to offer its new flagship as a saloon and Cabriolet, as well as in six-light Familiale and Limousine form. In the end, very few six-cylinder Cabriolets were built, making them much prized by collectors today, and no six-light Limousines were built after the war.

In 1947, the original 15 Six G engine, the letter 'G' – for 'Gauche' – denoting that the engine turned to the left, was replaced by the 15 Six D (for 'Droite'), which tuned to the right. A new gearbox, with a lower second-gear ratio, was fitted at the same time. In July 1952, the window frames were painted light grey.

The biggest change to the specification of the 15 Six, however, came late in its career, in 1954, when self-levelling hydropneumatic rear suspension was fitted to the 15 Six H (for

Period advertisement for the 15 Six. (Courtesy Citroën Communication)

Citroën Cars 1934 to 1986 – A Pictorial History

'Hydraulique'). It was a first on a production car, prefiguring the all-round hydraulic suspension, brakes, steering and gear change which would be fitted to the DS, introduced the following year. A lever in the boot allowed the driver to adjust the ride height, while a control on the dashboard made it possible to lock the rear suspension at the normal ride height when the car was parked. Twin rear lights were fitted to the 15 Six at this time, and the model badge at the rear was relocated in the centre.

The 15 Six H served as the basis for two special coachbuilt cars produced for René Coty, the President of France from

1954-1959. The first was a ceremonial limousine, designed by Philippe Charbonneaux and the last car built by the coachbuilder Franay in 1955. The second was a unique

Traction Avant

Smoky Grey (Gris Fumée) exclusive to the 15 Six from 1954.

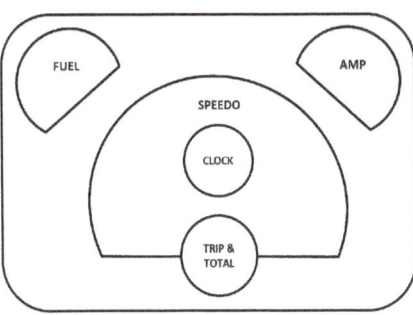

Dashboard layout of the 15 Six.

convertible created by Henri Chapron and delivered to the Elysée in 1956.

In total, only 3077 15 Six H cars were built, making it a sought-after model for Traction Avant enthusiasts today. Although by then an ageing design, the 15 Six had few rivals on France's 'Routes Nationales' in the early 1950s, where it was known as 'La reine de la route' (the queen of the road). Neither the DS, which succeeded it, nor the later CX ever received six-cylinder engines. The SM coupé launched in 1970 boasted a glorious Maserati V6, but it would be 1989 before a V6 engine would be installed in another Citroën saloon, the XM.

NUMBER PRODUCED: 50,602; years built: 1938-1955.
PRICE (1952): 859,920FF.
ENGINE: Water-cooled, six-cylinder petrol, longitudinally mounted with gearbox at front, OHV layout. Bore 78mm, stroke 100mm, capacity 2867cc, maximum power (15 Six D) 77bhp at 3800rpm, Solex 30 PAAI carburettor.
TRANSMISSION: Front-wheel drive, three-speed manual gearbox with synchromesh on second and third, dashboard-mounted selector. Final drive ratio: 3.875:1; gear ratios first: 3.42:1, second 1.45:1, third 1.00:1.
BRAKES: drums at front and rear, hydraulically operated.
TYRES: 185 X 400 (Michelin).
SUSPENSION: Front: independent, using longitudinal torsion bars and wishbone set-up; rear: beam axle with Panhard rod, trailing arms and transverse torsion bars. 15 Six H: hydropneumatic self-levelling at rear.
STEERING: Rack and pinion.
DIMENSIONS: Length: 4.76m (187.4in); width: 1.79m (70.5in); height: 1.56m (61.4in); wheelbase: 3.09m (121.7in); turning circle: 13.9m (45.5ft).
KERB WEIGHT: 3125kg (2921lb).
CAPACITIES: Fuel: 70l (15.4gal); boot (larger model): $0.23m^3$ ($8.1ft^3$).
COLOURS
Prewar: Body and wings: black (Noir) only, with ivory or red wheels.
1945-1952: Noir or Gris Irisé with ivory or (1946 only) red wheels.
1953-1954: Noir, Bleu RAF, Gris Perle and Bleu d'Islande, with colour of wheels depending on body colour.
1954-1957: Noir, Gris Perle, Bleu de Nuit, Gris Bruyère and Gris Fumée (unique to 15 Six), with grey or ivory wheels depending on body colour.

22CV

As early as 1934, Citroën mentioned a planned 22CV model in its publicity material. It was intended to be the ultimate Traction Avant variant (or 'Super Traction'), with a 3.8-litre V8 engine and a projected top speed of 140km/h (87mph).

Several running prototypes were assembled, early prototypes using Ford V8 engines. The cars reportedly had problems with their CV joints, but above all it came down to money, and Citroën could not afford to put the 22CV into production. It is believed that the prototypes were rebuilt with 11CV running gear, bonnets and front wings and sold off. A single V8-powered SM prototype was built in the 1970s, but no Citroën model ever made it into production with a V8 engine. In recent years, however, a number of 22CV replicas have been built by enthusiasts, some using Ford flathead V8 engines.

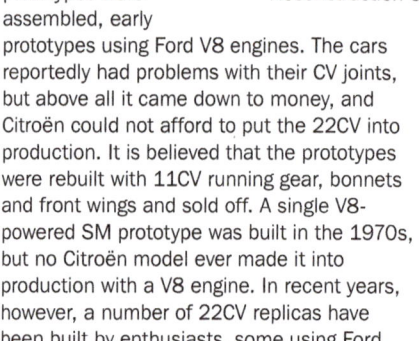

Reconstruction of a 22CV by a Dutch enthusiast.

Splendilux saloon conversion.

Conversions and special bodies

In the postwar years, France had a thriving market for car accessories, from Quillery steering wheels to Robergel wire wheels. The owner of a Traction Avant who wanted to personalise his or her car, however, could go much further.

Some companies like Tonneline or the Tôlerie Automobile Industrielle (TAI) offered extensive styling kits, with additional or replacement panels which could be fitted to an existing Traction Avant. TAI's Splendilux kit, for example, could be fitted to a saloon or Cabriolet; it comprised a new rounded radiator grille with vertical chrome slats, streamlined front wings with Marchal headlamps, a new bonnet, different stainless steel bumpers, an extended boot and teardrop-shaped rear wings with additional chrome trim. Meanwhile, the coachbuilder Robert Clabot offered to

Cabriolet conversions from Splendilux and Clabot.

Marius Renard cars on show in Lyon.

transform an existing Traction Avant roadster into 'Une voiture de grand luxe.'

After the war, Marius Renard modified about 20 Traction Avant cars – a mix of saloons, including a couple of 15 Six models, and convertibles – working together with the Citroën dealer Mézille from Puteaux (outside Paris); his modified cars were sold by Mézille and by Marchand in Lyon. We also owe a single rebodied Traction Avant roadster from 1938 to Renard et Bec; this had a completely redesigned front end reminiscent of some Delahaye and Alfa Romeo models. It is believed that this may have been styled by the famous motoring artist Géo Ham.

No official four-door Traction Avant convertibles were produced by Citroën, but some French coachbuilders – including EDM and AEAT– built a limited number of conversions. The two designs were very similar and both were marketed by Citroën in Belgium, immediately before and after the war.

Whether these conversions improved the looks of the standard cars is a matter of individual taste, but the rare survivors attract a great deal of interest when they are shown at classic car events.

1938 Renard et Bec 11CV 'Large' convertible.

One of the extremely rare four-door convertibles based on the Traction Avant.

Citroën Cars 1934 to 1986 – A Pictorial History

UK-built cars

Automobiles Citroën began selling cars in the UK in the very first year of its existence, and demand quickly grew. In 1923, it therefore established a subsidiary in Hammersmith (west London) to import and distribute its range of cars. The introduction by the British government of swingeing import duties on foreign vehicles – to protect its domestic manufacturers – led Citroën to set up a factory in Slough, to the west of the capital, in 1926, chiefly to build right-hand drive cars for sale in the UK and the Commonwealth. These had to have at least 51% British parts, which included items such as Lucas headlamps, Smiths instruments and Connolly leather upholstery, as well as UK-sourced glass and bumpers. All the UK cars had 12-volt electrics.

The Traction Avant was assembled in Slough throughout its career. Most body types were produced there (albeit with no Familiale models after the war), and the UK-built cars were typically more luxuriously finished than their French counterparts, with features such as a chrome radiator grille, sunroof, leather

UK magazine advertisement for the 'Super Modern Twelve' saloon.

seats and door cards, and wool headlining. A wider range of colours was offered than in France. The dashboards were finished in

Light Fifteen' Roadster from 1939.

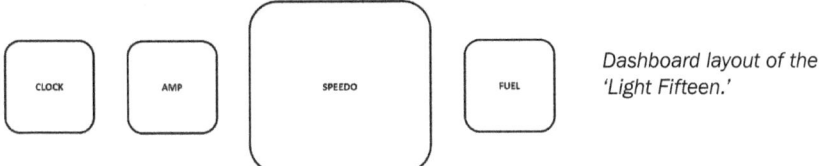

Dashboard layout of the 'Light Fifteen.'

wood veneer and the instrument layout was different, with more conventional twin round dials on the prewar 'Twelve' and rectangular dials on the 'Light Fifteen.' In both cases, these replaced the Jaeger instruments fitted to cars built in France.

Twelve? The cars destined for the UK market were given model names to reflect the British horsepower ratings then in force, which were calculated differently to those used in France. This makes for some confusing comparisons, with the original French 7CV referred to as the 'Twelve' (and even the 'Super Modern Twelve'), the 11 Légère and 11 Normale becoming the 'Light Fifteen' and 'Big Fifteen' respectively, and the French 15 Six known simply as the 'Big Six.'

In the UK market, the 'Super Modern Twelve' was priced at £250 in 1935 and the 'Fifteen' at £315. Twenty years later, in 1955, the price of the 'Big Six' had risen in the UK to £1474, including purchase tax.

The Slough-built 'Big Six' was quite an exclusive model, with only 1300 cars produced. Some of these were exported for sale in other right-hand drive markets such as Australia, New Zealand and South Africa. One famous British customer for the 'Big Six' was MIRA, the Motor Industry Research Association, based at Nuneaton, which used its 1952 car for instrumented testing work. The UK-built 15 Six H was the rarest version of all, with just 77 cars assembled at Slough: 7 in 1954 and 70 in 1955.

DS and ID

By the 1950s, the once radical Traction Avant was beginning to look rather long in the tooth. The launch of the 2CV in 1948 had been Citroën's immediate priority after the war, but in 1955 it was ready to create a fresh sensation at the Paris Motor Show. Like its predecessor, the DS – its name a play on the French word 'Déesse' (Goddess) – was a revolutionary design.

Its body was once again styled by Flaminio Bertoni, and its ultra-modern lines earned it the nickname of the 'flying saucer.' But it was also more efficient aerodynamically and its fibreglass roof lowered the car's centre of gravity, contributing to its excellent handling. In 1999, the magazine *Classic & Sports Car* voted it 'The Most Beautiful Car of All Time.' Inside, its dashboard – supposedly the largest nylon moulding in the world – was just as futuristic, and the DS introduced the single-spoke steering wheel which became a trademark of Citroën's cars.

It was the DS' technology and engineering, however, which really set the new car in a class of its own. This work was led by André Lefèbvre, with Paul Magès responsible for the car's hydraulic systems. At the end of the Traction Avant's career, Citroën had pioneered the use of self-levelling hydropneumatic rear

Celebrating the history of the DS at Rétromobile. (Courtesy Citroën Communication)

Cutaway model of a post-facelift DS 21 saloon.

26

DS and ID

The DS was honoured in a retrospective at the Paris Motor Show nearly 50 years after its launch.

suspension on the 15 Six H. For the DS it went much further, equipping the new model with a single hydraulic system for its suspension, steering, brakes and gear change.

For the first time, the DS featured all-round hydropneumatic suspension with automatic self-levelling and variable ground clearance. The constant ride height was an especially valuable feature on the estates, which were added to the range in 1958. The new suspension endowed the DS with its legendary 'magic carpet' ride, but also gave it an unrivalled level of active safety. When an assassination attempt was made on the French President Charles de Gaulle in 1962, his driver was famously able to escape at full speed, despite having two punctured tyres, and saved the President's life. The system used on the DS would be the basis for the advanced suspension on some nine million Citroëns, and was even licensed to Rolls-Royce for its Silver Shadow in 1965.

Citroën's new hydraulic systems took some getting used to. Its brakes were operated by a mushroom-like button on the floor, rather than a conventional pedal, and required minimal effort. Jaguar had demonstrated the effectiveness of disc brakes in competition on its C-Type from 1953, but the DS was the first mass-produced car to feature front disc brakes, giving it far superior stopping power.

The transmission was, in essence, a four-speed synchromesh gearbox with automatic operation of the clutch, using hydraulic power

operation. Rather than changing gear by means of a conventional floor gearlever, the driver used a finger-light control on top of the steering column, and there was no clutch pedal.

Only its engine somewhat let the side down. Financial pressures on the company meant that the DS launched with the ancient 1911cc four-cylinder engine dating back to 1934, admittedly the 11D variant fitted to the Traction Avant 11CV from 1955. Citroën had planned to develop an air-cooled flat-six engine for the DS but never had the money to see this into production.

The new model was initially as daunting for Citroën's mechanics as its first customers. The car suffered early reliability problems, not helped by a shortage of service information for its dealers. To reduce its reputation for complexity, however, and to offer a lower-priced entry model, in 1957 Citroën introduced

A 1959 Citroën ID 19 Break Luxe; one of the oldest still on the road.

Citroën Cars 1934 to 1986 – A Pictorial History

the ID. This had a simplified hydraulic system, with a conventional gearbox and brakes and unassisted steering, as well as a slightly less powerful engine.

Like the Traction Avant before it, the DS started out as a spacious four-door saloon, but evolved into a more extensive range. As well as the ID and estate models already mentioned, the DS served as the basis for a superbly elegant convertible, built by the French coachbuilder Henri Chapron. These convertibles are undoubtedly the most sought-after DS models on the classic car market today. Chapron – and some other smaller companies – produced a number of other versions of the DS with special bodywork.

By turns spacious or stylish, the DS also enjoyed success in motorsports like rallying, thanks to the top French drivers of their day such as Paul Coltelloni, Lucien Bianchi, René Trautmann and Bob Neyret. It won the Monte-Carlo Rally in 1959 and (controversially) 1966, the Tour de Corse in 1961 and 1963 and the Rallye du Maroc in 1969 and 1970. Initially, the cars used in rallying were similar to the production saloons, but with the rear wings cut away to allow faster wheel changes. Later in its career, however, special rallying versions were built on a shortened chassis with a two-door body. Some drivers preferred the tougher manual gearbox normally fitted to the ID, while others found the hydraulic change faster.

Altogether, 1,456,115 DS and ID cars were built, the largest number of these at Citroën's historic plant at the Quai de Javel in Paris. In addition, they were produced in Belgium (where nearly 100,000 cars were built), Portugal, Slovenia and South Africa, and even in Australia (home to the ID 19 Parisienne). Until 1965, they were assembled at Citroën's factory at Slough in the UK. The DS was sold in left-hand drive form in North America from 1956-1972, but it lacked the power and luxury features like air-conditioning or electric windows that American buyers expected. As with the SM, Citroën also faced regulatory problems in the USA with the headlamps fitted to post-facelift cars.

One of Chapron's 'works convertibles' on display at the Citromuseum in Castellane.

The production line at the Quai de Javel. (Courtesy Citroën Communication)

Short-wheelbase rally versions of the DS on show in front of the château at Chantilly.

DS saloon

When the DS was first shown to the public at the Paris Motor Show in autumn 1955, Citroën took 80,000 deposits in 10 days, a record that would allegedly only be broken – by the Tesla Model 3 – in 2016. The first cars were hand-built, and production only really got under way in February 1956. The very first cars from 1955-1957 can be recognised by their fishtail exhaust and so-called 'chip cone' rear indicators. Inside, plain jersey cloth was the only upholstery available, before patterned nylon fabric was offered as an alternative.

For the first restyle in August 1959, the DS received longer rear wings, and from 1959-1962 cooling grilles (for the hydraulic system) were fitted on top of the front wings. In March 1961, the 1911cc engine was uprated to 83bhp (SAE) at 4500rpm, thanks to a higher compression ratio, a new piston design, and a new twin-choke carburettor.

For the 1962 model year, Citroën redesigned the dashboard: it now looked more modern and was easier to use, as well as being cheaper to produce.

For the following model year (1963), the front of the car was slightly restyled, for improved aerodynamic efficiency and better cooling. Rubber bumper overriders were added. At the start of 1963, manual transmission – originally offered only on the cheaper ID – became available on the DS.

The 1965 model year saw a significant addition to Citroën's lexicon, when the Pallas trim level became available for the first time. Named after the Greek goddess Pallas Athena, the new version could be identified by its brushed aluminium door pillars, stainless steel sill trims, and full-length rubbing strips, as well a specific design of wheel trim. Additional long-range driving lamps, an option on other models, were fitted as standard, while Gris Palladium (a metallic grey) was a colour exclusive to the Pallas. Inside, the doors were fully padded and had additional aluminium trim. There was a deep Dunlopillo underlay to the carpets, improving soundproofing and adding to the feel of luxury. The front seat backrests were taller, and leather upholstery (in black or tan) was optional, together with a front central armrest. The cloth headlining was new. The DS Prestige was also added to the range at this time: intended for official use and chauffeur-driven cars, it had a glass panel between the front and rear compartments.

An early DS 19 saloon.

Citroën Cars 1934 to 1986 – A Pictorial History

The 32nd DS built; believed to be the oldest survivor.

DS 19 (1955-1965)

NUMBER PRODUCED: 1,456,115 (all DS and ID models).
PRICE AT LAUNCH: 965,000FF.
ENGINE: Water-cooled, four-cylinder petrol, OHV layout. Bore 78mm, stroke 100mm, capacity 1911cc, maximum power 75bhp (SAE) at 4500rpm until 03/1961, then 83bhp (SAE) at 4500rpm, Weber 24/30 carburettor until 03/1961, then Weber 24/32.
TRANSMISSION: Front-wheel drive, hydraulically operated semi-automatic with four forward speeds and no clutch pedal, steering column-mounted selector. Four-speed manual gearbox with conventional clutch optional from January 1963. Final drive ratio: 3.89:1; gear ratios: first 3.55:1, second 1.89:1, third 1.23:1, fourth 0.85:1.
BRAKES: Front: inboard discs; rear: outboard drums. Hydraulic servo control and dual circuits.
TYRES: 165 x 400 Michelin X radial.
SUSPENSION: Fully independent self-levelling hydropneumatic, with leading arms at front

Original dashboard design. (Courtesy Citroën Communication)

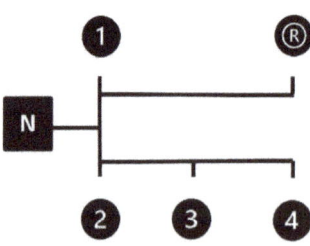

Gear change layout for the hydraulic transmission.

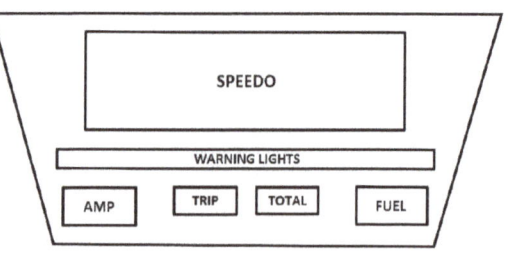

DS and ID

Revised dashboard design from 1962 onwards (photo shows convertible).

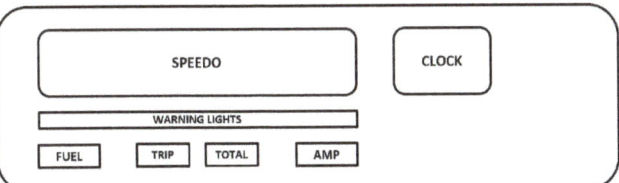

In 1965, the 'Pallas' moved the DS upmarket. Customers could choose cloth or leather upholstery. (Both photos courtesy Citroën Communication)

and trailing arms at rear. Anti-roll bars at front and rear.
STEERING: Rack and pinion, with hydraulic power assistance.
DIMENSIONS: Length: 4.80m (189.0in); width: 1.82m (71.7in); height: 1.47m (57.9in); wheelbase: 3.12m (122.8in); turning circle: 11.0m (36.1ft).
KERB WEIGHT: 1310kg (2888lb).

CAPACITIES: Fuel: 60l (13.2gal); boot: 0.48m^3 (17.0ft^3).
COLOURS (1956): Noir, Champagne, Vert Printemps, Aubergine, Gris Rosé. The range extended each year with different shades of grey, blue and brown, as well as yellow and red

(in all, 218 colours were offered during the DS' career!).

The next two years saw a number of technical changes to the DS. In September 1965, a short-stroke five-bearing 1985cc engine replaced the venerable 1911cc unit. This model was initially known as the DS 19A (or DS 19MA when fitted with a manual gearbox). Alongside these models, Citroën further enlarged the capacity of the engine to 2175cc to create the DS 21.

In 1966, a new mineral oil-based fluid known as LHM ('Liquide Hydraulique Minéral') was introduced for the car's hydraulic systems: this was much less harsh on the car's components but required completely different seals. The LHM fluid was dyed green and components such as the suspension spheres painted green to prevent any risk of confusion. Finally, in September 1967 the dynamo was replaced by an alternator.

The 1968 model year saw the most radical change to the styling of the DS, which was by then 12 years old. Citroën's in-house designer Robert Opron completely updated the look of the car by redesigning the front wings and fitting a pair of headlamps under a transparent cover; the inner pair of lamps were connected to the steering by means of cables, and could turn up to 80°. The improvement when cornering at night on country roads is something we take for granted with today's directional LED headlamps, but was a major innovation at the time.

For the following model year (1969), the engine line-up was revised: the DS 21 now developed 115bhp (SAE), while the DS 19A evolved into the DS 20 as its power output increased significantly to 103bhp (SAE). A heated rear window and front centre armrest could now be specified as options, as could a radio with a black frame (matching the revised finish of the dashboard).

In September 1969, however, the DS' dashboard was completely redesigned and for the first time it sported three round dials, including a rev counter. What it lost in character, it made up for in its improved functionality. The third major design of dashboard used by Citroën, it was fitted to the DS until the end of its career. At the same time, the DS moved further upmarket, when Bosch Jetronic fuel-injection became available on the DS 21 IE (for 'injection électronique'). Power rose to 139bhp (SAE) and Citroën's

Facelifted models can be easily recognised by their revised frontal treatment.

DS and ID

This DS 20 Pallas sports rear window blinds: a period accessory.

new flagship could reach a top speed of 188km/h (117mph).

Its successful facelift and continued mechanical improvements gave the DS a new lease of life and it recorded its highest ever production figure in 1970, when over 103,000 cars were built. Its story was not yet completely told, however: in September 1970, a five-speed manual gearbox became available on the DS 21 and D Super 5, as France started to build out its network of autoroutes. This was followed in December 1971 by a three-speed Borg Warner automatic.

Directional headlamps arrived with the DS' facelift for 1968. (Courtesy Citroën Communication)

DS 19A and DS 20 (1965-1971)

KEY DIFFERENCES
ENGINE: Bore 86mm, stroke 85.5mm, capacity 1985cc, maximum power 90bhp (SAE) at 5250rpm from 1965-1968, then 103bhp (SAE) at 5250rpm, Weber 28/36 carburettor.
TRANSMISSION: Hydraulically operated semi-automatic with four forward speeds and no clutch pedal, or four-speed manual gearbox with conventional clutch.
COLOURS (1968): Blanc Carrare, Bleu Angora, Vert Ilicinée, Gris Nocturne, Bleu Andalou, Rouge Corsaire, Bordeaux, Gris Palladium, Gris Kandahar.

Final dashboard design for the DS, introduced for 1970. (Courtesy Citroën Communication)

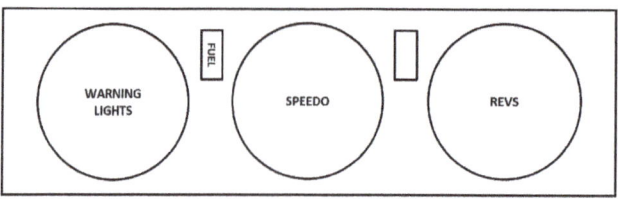

DS 21 (1965-1972)

KEY DIFFERENCES
ENGINE: Bore 90mm, stroke 85.5mm, capacity 2175cc, maximum power 109bhp (SAE) at 5500rpm from 1965-1968, then 115bhp (SAE)/106bhp (DIN) at 5750rpm, Weber 28/36 carburettor. (DS 21 IE: maximum power 139bhp (SAE)/125bhp (DIN) at 5500rpm, Bosch Jetronic electronic fuel-injection.)
TRANSMISSION: Hydraulically operated semi-automatic with four forward speeds and no clutch pedal, or manual gearbox with conventional clutch (four-speed until 1970, then five-speed). Three-speed Borg Warner fully automatic gearbox optional from December 1971. Steering column-mounted selector or gearlever in all cases. Four-speed manual: Final drive ratio: 4.375:1; gear ratios: first 3.25:1; second 1.94:1; third 1.28:1; fourth 0.85:1.
DIMENSIONS (post-facelift model): Length: saloon 4.87m (191.7in), convertible 4.90m (192.9in); height: saloon 1.47m (57.9in), convertible 1.44m (56.7in).

KERB WEIGHT: 1350kg (2976lb).
COLOURS (1971): Noir, Blanc Meije, Bleu Platine, Vert Charmille, Bronze, Sable Métallisé, Gris d'Anjou, Bordeaux, Gris Nacré, Rouge de Rio, Beige Albatros, Bleu Camargue.

DS 23 (1973-1975)

Finally, for the 1973 model year, the DS 23 replaced the DS 21. It was sold in carburettor or fuel-injected form, producing 115bhp (DIN) and 130bhp (DIN) respectively, with the choice of three transmissions: four-speed hydraulic, five-speed manual or three-speed automatic. A handful of cars were built with a five-speed hydraulic transmission, but this was not generally available. As on the DS 21, Confort and Pallas trims were available, but the latter again proved more popular, especially on the fuel-injected version. Air-conditioning was available as an option; cars fitted with it had an additional grille let into the front valance. Production of the DS came to an end in April 1975, but the

DS and ID

new CX was initially sold only as a 2000 or 2200 with significantly less power, and Citroën's customers would have to wait for the CX 2400 GTi in 1977 before they could enjoy the same level of performance.

KEY DIFFERENCES
ENGINE: Bore 93.5mm, stroke 85.5mm, capacity 2347cc, maximum power 124bhp (SAE)/115bhp (DIN) at 5500rpm, Weber 28/36 carburettor. (DS 23 IE: maximum power 141bhp (SAE)/130bhp (DIN) at 5500rpm,

Bosch Jetronic electronic fuel-injection.)
TRANSMISSION: Hydraulically operated semi-automatic with four (or five) forward speeds and no clutch pedal, or five-speed manual gearbox with conventional clutch, or three-speed Borg Warner fully automatic gearbox. Steering column-mounted selector or gearlever in all cases.
COLOURS (1974): Beige Vanneau, Blanc Meije, Bleu Lagune, Ivoire Borély, Noir, Beige Tholonet, Bleu Delta, Brun Scarabée, Gris Nacré, Vert Argenté.

1974 DS 23 IE Pallas. (Courtesy Citroën Communication)

1967 ID 19 in Bordeaux Red with black roof.

ID saloon

The ID 19 Luxe was first shown at the Paris Motor Show in autumn 1956 and went on sale the following May, finally replacing the Traction Avant 11CV. The name was a play on the French word 'idée' (idea). It had a simplified hydraulic system, with a conventional manual gearbox (with no synchromesh on first) and brakes, and unassisted steering. The engine was

35

Citroën Cars 1934 to 1986 – A Pictorial History

slightly less powerful than the unit fitted to the DS 19, producing 66bhp (SAE). It was cheaper to buy and easier to adapt to for existing Traction Avant owners; it proved popular with more traditional customers and high-mileage drivers (including taxis).

Externally, the ID could be distinguished from the DS by its small hubcaps and aluminium bumpers The roof, made from reinforced resin, was initially translucent, but from 1961-1969, all IDs had a white roof regardless of the body colour. The rear screen was made from plexiglass rather than glass until 1963, when glass was standardised on all DS and ID saloons. Several parts of the body were painted: the door pillars and sills, the headlamp rims and front valance. Throughout the ID's career, the double chevron on the boot lid was silver, rather than gold as on the DS. Inside, the steering wheel was larger, to compensate for the lack of power assistance, and the dashboard was a simpler, metal affair. The gear change was column-mounted and there was a conventional brake pedal. The boot trim was more basic, with a simple metal rod to hold it open instead of the struts on the DS.

The ID range was soon extended. A more luxurious ID 19 Confort model was introduced in 1957 and quickly became the best-selling model. This had the more comfortable seats from the DS, carpets, heating ducts for the rear passengers and extra equipment including a clock. A 'Voiture de Maître' with a glass division between the front and rear compartments also became available. At the other extreme, in October 1957, the ID 19 Normale was added, to appeal to Traction Avant owners who still found the ID 19 too expensive. This had a bench seat in the front, simplified instrumentation and a steel (rather than aluminium) bonnet. The engine, carried over from the Traction Avant, produced only 62bhp (SAE). It was not a success and only 400 cars were sold before it was withdrawn.

Over the next few years, the gap in equipment and performance between the DS and ID gradually narrowed. In 1958, chrome headlamp trims were fitted; the following year, the ID gained larger wheel trims and aluminium-finished door pillars. In 1960, 12-volt electrics were added, while power-assisted brakes and telescopic boot struts arrived in 1961. In 1962, power-assisted steering was a welcome addition to the options list; cars fitted with it had a thinner-rimmed steering wheel. The power output of the ID steadily increased during the 1960s. For the 1965 model year, power on the ID saloons went up to 75bhp (SAE), and a year later, for the 1966 model year, the 83bhp (SAE) engine from the DS 19 was fitted. This only lasted a year, however, as in September 1966 Citroën installed a de-tuned version of its new 1985cc engine, initially producing 84bhp (SAE), increasing in 1968 to 91bhp.

Late-model D Super 5. (Courtesy Citroën Communication)

DS and ID

The major facelift of the DS for the 1968 model year was also applied to the ID. Although all IDs now had twin headlamps, the swivelling inner pair could only be specified as an option on cars fitted with power steering. A notable customer for the ID that year was the French Gendarmerie Nationale, which acquired three ID saloons to a unique specification, with 2175cc engines with a Roots-type supercharger. Developing an estimated 150bhp, these were the most powerful DS/ID cars ever built. More prosaically, in 1969 a new model, the ID 20, was introduced: this was fitted with the 103bhp (SAE) engine from the DS 20 and was sold only in Confort trim.

For 1970, however, the entire ID range was overhauled: the ID 19 was replaced by the D Spécial and the ID 20 by the D Super, the latter developing 103bhp (SAE). Both models received the same three-dial dashboard as the DS. A year later, a five-speed gearbox could be specified on the D Super. In 1972, both the D Spécial and D Super received a final hike in power, to 108bhp (SAE). The range was reconfigured again in 1973, when the D Super 5 was launched with the 2175cc engine from the DS 21 and a standard five-speed gearbox. The five-speed option on the 'regular' D Super was dropped at the same time. The D Super 5 was the first of the ID's descendants to go out of production, in January 1975, followed soon afterwards by the D Spécial and D Super.

ID (1957-1969)

KEY DIFFERENCES
NUMBER PRODUCED: 445,000.
ENGINE: Bore 78mm, stroke 100mm, capacity 1911cc, maximum power 66bhp (SAE) at 4500rpm until 1964, then 75bhp (SAE) at 4500rpm for 1964-1965 and 83bhp (SAE) for 1965-1966, Solex 34 PBIC carburettor. From 1966: Bore 86mm, stroke 85.5mm, capacity 1985cc, maximum power 84bhp (SAE) at 5250rpm, then 91bhp (SAE) from 1968, Solex 34 PBIC carburettor.
TRANSMISSION: Four-speed manual gearbox, with synchromesh on top three ratios only until 1963.
STEERING: Rack and pinion, with hydraulic power assistance optional from 1962.
BRAKES: Front: inboard discs; rear: outboard drums, unassisted until 1961 and operated by conventional foot pedal.
KERB WEIGHT: 1120kg (2469lb).
COLOURS (1959): Noir, Écaille Blonde, Bleu Nuage, Marron Glacé, Gris Mirage, Bleu Nuit.

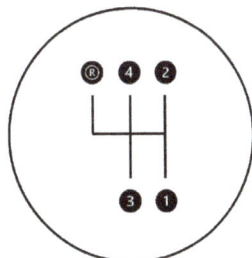

ID gear change layout.

Estates

After the Familiale and Commerciale versions of the Traction Avant, it was a logical step for Citroën to introduce an estate version of the ID in 1958. The model was known by different names in the different markets in which it was sold: 'Break' in France, 'Safari' and Estate' in the UK, 'Station

1959 ID 19 Break.

Citroën Cars 1934 to 1986 – A Pictorial History

Providing support on the long-distance rally from Paris to Kabul in 1970. (Courtesy Citroën Communication)

To cope with the greater loads the estate would carry, it had larger rear brake drums and the braking system from the DS. The final drive ratio was lowered to provide better acceleration when loaded. In 1963, the estates were fitted with the more powerful 83bhp engine from the DS, two years before it became available in the ID saloon.

All models had a two-piece folding tailgate with a second rear number plate that could be seen when the lower section was folded down to carry longer items. The roof was made from steel, in order to support the weight of items on the cars' standard-fit roof rack.

A range of different seating options was available. In the front, customers could choose between a pair of separate seats or a bench, the latter making it possible to carry six passengers. The standard Break/Safari models had a conventional folding bench seat in the middle and two occasional, side-facing seats in the rear, which could be folded into the floor when not in use.

The rarer Familiale version had three folding seats in the middle and a fixed bench in row three; this layout required moving the fuel tank further to the rear. Finally, the ID Commerciale model – which was offered in a single trim level (Luxe) – had vinyl upholstery and two

Wagon' in the US and 'Safari' or 'Station Wagon' in Australia.

Its hydropneumatic suspension was ideally suited to heavy loads: the car could be lowered to its lowest setting for ease of loading, and would maintain a constant ride height, whatever its cargo. The suspension was very compact, making for a low, flat floor to the load deck. It even provided a steady platform for the patients who were transported in the ambulance versions often used in France, and for camera crews, including those of the BBC.

All DS and ID estates had a two-section rear tailgate.

Note the second number plate, visible when driving with the lower section of the tailgate open.

DS and ID

The loading arrangements demonstrated on a DS 20 Break. (Courtesy Paul Buckett)

Late-model DS 23 Break.

bench seats in the front and middle; the latter could be folded down, as on the Break/Safari. This was the rarest variant of all, with just 500 cars built each year.

Two styles of ambulance body were available, with either a standard or elevated roof, with conversions available from the factory or from several French coachbuilders, including Baboulin, Delorme, Filca, Petit and Currus (later absorbed into Gruau). The rear compartment was arranged to accommodate a stretcher with a nurse seated alongside the patient.

Broadly speaking, the estate models followed the major changes made to the ID saloons, including the major facelift for the 1968 model year. The most powerful engine fitted was the 2347cc unit from the DS 23 saloon, in carburettor form only, offered from 1972 until the end of production in 1975.

ID/DS estate

NUMBER PRODUCED: 94,044.
DIMENSIONS: Length: 5.02m (197.8in); width: 1.82m (71.5in); height: 1.53m (60.2in).
KERB WEIGHT: 1400kg (3086lb).
CAPACITIES: Fuel: 65l (14.3gal); boot: (max.) 2.01m^3 (71.0ft^3).

Gear change layout for a 1971 UK-market Safari 21.

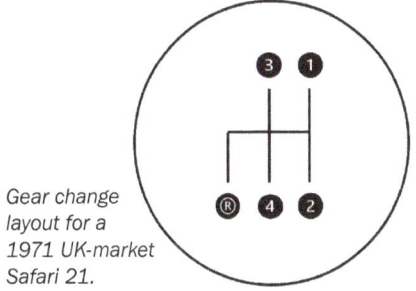

Works convertibles

For many DS enthusiasts, the most desirable models of all are the convertibles, conceived and built by the French coachbuilder Henri Chapron. Chapron established his business on the outskirts of Paris in 1919, and created special bodies for the major French luxury makes during the 1920s and 1930s. After the war, even though mass production and monocoque bodies became the norm, he managed to keep going. In 1958, he turned his attention to the DS, creating two cabriolets: a four-seat version which became 'La Croisette,' and the two-seat 'Le Caddy.' The 'La Croisette' was developed quite independently from Citroën, and was by no means perfect: the first cars had a vertical chrome strip masking what would have been the join between the wing and the rear door on the saloon.

It wowed the crowds at the Paris Motor Show in 1958, and Citroën and Chapron agreed to collaborate and build a production version, the so-called 'Décapotable Usine' (works convertible). This was launched in 1960 and sold through Citroën's dealer network until 1971. Flaminio Bertoni proposed a much more harmonious design with a single-piece rear wing: this was used for Chapron's own 'La Croisette' model from 1960-1962, as well as the works convertible. Early cars used the floorpan from the saloon, cars built from 1964 that from the estate. Before the facelift for the 1968 model year, Pichon Parat offered a different set of front wings with twin headlamps (fixed, rather than swivelling).

The 'Décapotable Usine' was available in both DS and ID form, but in practice, most

1961 Citroen DS 19 'La Croisette.'

1964 DS 19 works convertible. (Courtesy Bonhams)

DS and ID

Pre-facelift 'works convertible' by Chapron.

Post-facelift 'works convertible,' again by Chapron.

Interior of a 1964 DS 19 'works convertible.' (Courtesy Bonhams)

cars were based on the DS, generally on the most powerful version available at the time. They often had leather upholstery and many cars were equipped with the optional Jaeger dashboard with a series of small round dials. An electrically operated hood and a (very expensive) removable hardtop were available as extras. Altogether 1365 cars were built, the last of them a DS 21 IE.

DIMENSIONS (post-facelift model): Length: 4.90m (192.9in); width: 1.79m (70.5in); height: 1.44m (56.7in)

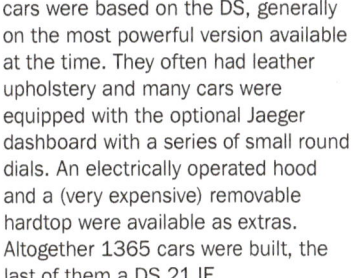

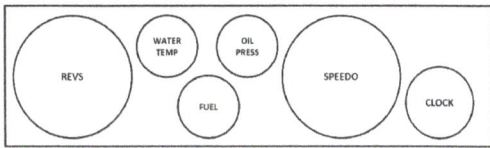

Layout of dashboard with Jaeger instruments.

41

Citroën Cars 1934 to 1986 – A Pictorial History

Other special bodies

Although Chapron is best known for the 'Décapotable Usine,' he produced a surprisingly wide range of special bodies for the DS, albeit in small numbers (with 50 or fewer examples of each model built). As well as 'La Croisette' (1958-1962) and 'Le Caddy' (1959-1968), he produced a third convertible model, 'Le Palm Beach' (1962-1972).

At the same time as 'La Croisette,' Chapron designed his first DS-based coupé, 'Le Paris,' but this was only sold in 1958 and 1959. Three more two-door coupés followed, however: 'Le Concorde' (1960-1965), 'Le Dandy' (1960-1968) and 'Le Léman' (1967-1974).

Chapron also produced two four-door saloons with different, more upright bodywork: 'La Majesty' (1965-1970) and then 'La Lorraine' (1970-1974). These had special exterior trim and luxuriously appointed interiors; a divider between the chauffeur and passenger compartment was available, as was armour-plating and bulletproof glass.

Last but not least, in 1968 Chapron produced an imposing one-off limousine, 'La

Pre- and post-facelift versions of 'Le Caddy.'

Pre-facelift version of 'Le Palm Beach.'

42

DS and ID

'Le Paris' coupé with early 'La Croisette' convertible beside it: note vertical chrome strips on both models.

'Le Concorde' coupé from 1963.

Above and right: 'Le Dandy' coupé.

Late-model 'Le Léman' coupé.

'La Majesty' saloon.

'La Lorraine' saloons; the right-hand car has bulletproof glass and armour-plating.

'La Présidentielle' limousine.

Présidentielle,' for use by de Gaulle. Much longer than the standard cars at 6.53m (257.1in), it had an occasional rearward-facing occasional seat in the rear compartment for use by an aide. De Gaulle apparently disliked the divider behind the driver, however, and preferred the old Traction Avant-based convertible or a standard DS saloon with a sunroof in which he could stand up when passing crowds.

While Chapron was undoubtedly the best-known coachbuilder to work with Citroën on the DS, he was not the only one. Heuliez proposed a four-door cabriolet, but this was rejected by Citroën on the grounds that it lacked rigidity. The German coachbuilder Reutter, more commonly associated with Porsche, also developed a four-door cabriolet and a few of these were actually built. In northern France, Hector Bossaert, the owner of the coachwork firm Gété, commissioned the Italian stylist Pietro Frua to design a two-door coupé on a shortened saloon chassis. The 1911cc engine was uprated and reputedly produced over 100bhp. Altogether, about a dozen examples of the Bossaert DS 19 GT are thought to have been built.

This section would not be complete without mentioning one other exceptional vehicle based on the DS: Michelin's extraordinary DS PLR (for 'Poids Lourd Rapide'), better known as the 'Mille Pattes' (or 'Centipede'). The 'Mille Pattes' was built in 1972 for use

A few coachbuilders attempted four-door convertible versions of the DS, but none proved successful.

The Bossaert DS 19 GT.

at Michelin's test track at Ladoux in the Auvergne. A massive 7.2m (283.5in) long and 2.45m (96.5in) wide, it had ten road wheels and was powered by two Chevrolet V8 engines: one to propel the car and the other to drive a sample tyre in the middle of the vehicle. This could be set up in multiple positions and tested at speeds of up to 180km/h (112mph).

The famous 'Mille Pattes.' (Courtesy Michelin)

Citroën Cars 1934 to 1986 – A Pictorial History

UK-built cars

As it had done with the Traction Avant and 2CV, until the end of 1965 Citroën assembled DS and ID saloons and estates at Slough, west of London, in order to avoid paying import duties. Altogether, some 8668 cars were built in the UK. The convertibles sold in the UK were all built in France, and after the factory at Slough closed, Citroën imported the saloons and estates too.

The Slough cars used a number of locally sourced components, including Lucas lights (with a different design at the rear from the French-built cars) and round Smiths instruments on all but the early cars. All UK-built cars used 12-volt electrics, supplied by Lucas until 1962. All the DS and ID cars assembled in Slough had right-hand drive and a mushroom-type brake pedal, but a conventional handbrake instead of the French cars' foot-operated parking brake. There were minor differences in exterior trim too, sometimes – as for the front number plate support – to conform to UK regulations. The biggest differences, however, were inside: both the DS and ID were positioned more upmarket, with leather upholstery and a wooden dashboard.

The ID Break was sold in the UK as the ID 19 Safari, and even this had the wooden dash, leather trim and the full-size wheel trims reserved for the DS in France. The Familiale was rechristened the 'Tourmaster.' Ambulance and hearse ('Cortège') models were offered by Citroën in the UK, while Harold Radford, known for its shooting brake conversions of many British cars, marketed a 'Countryman' version of the estate.

The most interesting model produced in the UK was probably the DW, launched in 1963. Positioned between the ID and DS models, this was the first DS anywhere in the world to combine the engine, power steering and brakes from the DS with manual transmission, until then fitted only to the ID.

Period advertisement in the UK. (Courtesy Citroën Communication)

A Slough-built DS returns to France. Note the different rear lights.

Another UK market special was developed by Connaught, in Surrey, which sold an upgrade for the 1911cc engine with twin SU or Solex carburettors in the early 1960s. Connaught also offered an interior package for the ID with the dashboard from the DS, reclining bucket seats and a three-spoke 'Stirling Moss' steering wheel. Later, the company sold complete cars as the Connaught GT, producing about 200 vehicles in all.

Citroën Cars 1934 to 1986 – A Pictorial History

CX

'Projet L' preserved at the Conservatoire Citroën.

Development work for the successor to the DS began in the late 1960s, soon after the successful facelift of the DS. Robert Opron led the design team for what was known internally as 'Projet L,' a large four-door saloon with aerodynamic lines. Several versions were considered, some inspired by the SM, at least one other with a hatchback. In the end, a three-box layout was chosen, with a low boot opening. It had a distinctive concave rear screen and a single windshield wiper. The interior, conceived by Michel Harmand, introduced the drum-like speedo and rev counter, and satellite controls that would be featured on a number of other models.

Several mechanical configurations were envisaged, including an air-cooled flat-six and a 1654cc water-cooled flat-four. This was the time when Maserati was part of Citroën and when the company was also looking at rotary power (as trialled in the M35 and fitted to the GS Birotor). The engine bay was therefore designed to accommodate the Maserati V6 from the SM, as well as two- and three-rotor Wankel engines. The plan to install a rotary engine was cancelled due to concerns about the high fuel consumption and poor sales of the GS Birotor, as well as the reliability issues experienced by NSU with its Ro80. In the end, the CX launched in August 1974 with the tried and tested four-cylinder petrol engines from the DS range. The engines were, however, installed transversely and inclined to the front, freeing up more space inside the car, even though it was shorter than the DS. Later, a new generation of petrol engines arrived and, for the first time, Citroën's big saloon became available with diesel power.

Following the success of the DS and ID estates, an estate version of the CX soon followed the saloon, in October 1975. The range also gradually expanded with the more powerful GTi models, as well as long-wheelbase saloons. This time, however, Citroën did not offer an official convertible model, and only a small number of special bodies were produced based on the CX.

The CX – its name a reference to the French

Advertisement for the CX at its launch in the UK. (Courtesy Citroën Communication)

CX

Facelifted saloon and estate in the foreground, with pre-facelift models behind them.

symbol c_x for drag coefficient – was the last car Robert Opron designed for the company, and the last all-new Citroën before it was taken over by Peugeot. It certainly got off to a flying start, when it was voted European Car of the Year 1975. Built in a brand-new factory at Aulnay-sous-Bois just outside Paris, annual sales soon exceeded 100,000. At different stages in its lifetime, the CX was also produced at Mangualde (Portugal), Vigo (Spain), and Arica (Chile). It was never officially sold in the United States, however, its variable-height suspension falling victim to American legislation.

The Traction Avant and DS were hard acts to follow, and in some respects the CX was less revolutionary than its predecessors. The hydraulic gear change from the DS was dropped and the only transmission available at launch was a conventional four-speed manual. The CX nonetheless retained the company's famous hydropneumatic suspension, now attached to subframes with flexible mountings to the body to further improve ride quality and reduce road noise. It had disc brakes all round, which was still quite unusual on a mainstream car in 1974, and used the same variable power assistance for its steering as the SM. In its early years, the CX achieved some success in competition, including a class win in the 1976 Morocco Rally, and a spirited third place overall for Paddy Hopkirk in the 1977 London–Sydney Marathon.

CX saloon rebuilt in the colours of the car entered in the 1978 Monte-Carlo Rally.

Citroën Cars 1934 to 1986 – A Pictorial History

CX saloon: Series 1

In the wake of the 1973 oil crisis, fuel economy was a key selling point for the new range, and the CX launched as the 2000 with the 1985cc engine; the 2000 Eco version used the same engine, but had a longer final drive ratio and top gear. These were joined in January 1975 by the 2200 model, known as the Club, with the more powerful 2175cc engine. The DS continued in production for a few months and the CX was positioned between the D Super and the DS 23 and DS 23 IE Pallas models, which had no immediate replacements. Production of right-hand drive cars began in 1975.

The CX 2000 came with halogen headlamps, a heated rear window, and driver's seat height

The CX 2000 at launch in 1974. (Courtesy Citroën Communication)

adjustment; the 2200 Club added thicker carpets, inertia-reel front seatbelts, front electric windows, and a rev counter (all of which were optional on the 2000), as well as an oil level gauge, air horn, additional warning lights, and map pockets in the front seat backrests. Externally, the 2200 Club could be identified by its full disc wheel trims and stainless steel exhaust tailpipe. Both cars started off with a four-speed manual gearbox and, perhaps surprisingly, unassisted steering, with power assistance an option. Metallic paint, tinted glass, head restraints and a radio were also listed as options for both models.

In July 1975, the range was revised. The basic model was now designated the Confort, while the Club was replaced by the Super, available in 2000 and 2200 form, which would become the best-selling version. It had

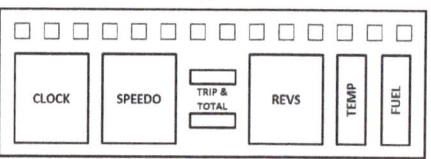

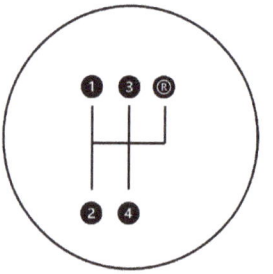

Dashboard and gear change layout for the CX.

smaller wheel trims than the Club. Inside, a pair of circular air vents was added to the centre console. Above these two trim levels, Citroën introduced the more luxurious Pallas model and, at the top of the range, the 2400 Prestige. Apart from the very first cars built, the Pallas can be recognised by the star-shaped design of the wheel trims used until 1977, as well as rubber inserts in the front bumper and chrome side rubbing strips. Inside, the Pallas gained velour upholstery and stainless steel sill plates.

The Prestige was built on a 25cm (10in) longer wheelbase than the standard saloons; some cars used by the Elysée also had a raised roofline, and this feature was made standard on all Prestige models for the 1978 model year. The Prestige was initially powered by the 2347cc carburettor-fed engine from the DS 23, developing 115bhp. Standard equipment included power steering, air-conditioning, front and rear electric windows and rear passenger footrests; cloth or leather upholstery was available, and a vinyl roof and alloy wheels were optional. The Prestige was used by the French Presidents Valéry Giscard d'Estaing and Jacques Chirac, as well as the East German leader Erich Honecker. Citroën even offered a 'Haute Protection' version of the Prestige, with armour-plated bodywork, reinforced brakes and suspension, and special glass.

In January 1976, the CX 2200D joined the range as Citroën's first diesel-engined car. It was powered by a 'dieselised' version of the 2175cc engine that had already been used in the C35 van; in this application, it developed 66bhp. On the petrol-engined CX 2200, a three-speed semi-automatic transmission known as C-matic became available as an option. A few months later, in July 1976, the 2347cc carburettor engine replaced the 2175cc unit and there were minor changes to the trim on all models.

The next big change came in May 1977, when Citroën introduced the CX 2400 GTi with the 2347cc engine from the DS 23. For the

Pre-1977 CX Pallas showing the distinctive star-shaped wheel trims.

Citroën Cars 1934 to 1986 – A Pictorial History

Pre-facelift CX Prestige.

first time since the DS 23 IE had gone out of production, fuel-injection (in this case, Bosch L-Jetronic) was available on the company's flagship. Maximum power was quoted at 128bhp (DIN) and was transmitted through a five-speed manual gearbox. The 2400 GTi could be recognised by its black window frames and door handles, and standard front fog lamps; the distinctive alloy wheels, initially optional, were soon made standard. Inside, there was a new, more supportive design of front seat with integrated headrests. Cars produced after 1980 had a rear spoiler.

In 1977, the fuel-injected engine and five-speed gearbox also made their way into the Prestige, and the five-speed manual transmission became an option on all 2400 models. In December that year, the CX 2400 Pallas Injection mated the fuel-injected engine to the C-matic semi-automatic transmission and standard power steering to create a model which was particularly luxurious and easy to drive.

1978 would be the most successful year ever for the CX, with just over 150,000 cars sold. In January, the diesel was enlarged to 2500cc and power increased to 75bhp. Six months later, a five-speed manual gearbox became an option. In May, a new heating system was fitted to all CX models and the centre console was redesigned, with a unique spherical ashtray mounted on top of it.

Trio of CX 2400 GTis in Bleu Régate, Orange Mandarine, and Vert Papyrus.

CX

CX 2000 and 2200 (1974-1979)

NUMBER PRODUCED: 150,598 (2000); 75,479 (2200).
PRICE AT LAUNCH: 25,785FF (2200: 30,768FF).
ENGINE: Water-cooled, four-cylinder petrol, transversely mounted, OHV layout. Bore 86mm (2200: 90mm), stroke 85.5mm, capacity 1985cc (2200: 2175cc), maximum power 102bhp (DIN) at 5500rpm (2200: 112bhp (DIN) at 5500rpm), Weber 34 DM TR 25 twin-choke carburettor.
TRANSMISSION: Front-wheel drive, four-speed manual gearbox with synchromesh on all gears, floor-mounted gearlever. Final drive ratio: 4.77:1 (2000 Eco: 4.36:1; 2200: 4.58:1; gear ratios: first 3.17:1; second 1.83:1; third 1.13:1; fourth 0.80:1 (2000 Eco: 0.75:1); 31.0km/h (19.3mph) per 1000rpm in top (2200: 32.2km/h/20.0mph). Three-speed C-matic semi-automatic transmission with floor-mounted selector optional on 2200. Final drive ratio: 4.77:1; gear ratios: first 1.94:1; second 1.13:1; third 0.80:1.
BRAKES: Front: ventilated discs; rear: solid discs. Hydraulic servo control and dual circuits.
TYRES: Front: 185 SR 14 (2200: HR-rated); rear: 175 SR 14 (2200: HR-rated).
SUSPENSION: Fully independent self-levelling hydropneumatic, with front wishbones and rear trailing arms. Anti-roll bars at front and rear.
STEERING: Rack and pinion, with optional 'Varipower' hydraulic power assistance.
DIMENSIONS: Length: 4.63m (182.3in); width: 1.73m (68.2in); height: 1.36m (53.5in); wheelbase: 2.845m (112.0in); turning circle (between kerbs): 10.8m (35.5ft).
KERB WEIGHT: 1265kg/2789lb (2200: 1285kg/2833lb).
CAPACITIES: Fuel: 68l (15.0gal); boot: 0.475m³ (16.9ft³).

CX 2400 Prestige (Series 1)

KEY DIFFERENCES
NUMBER PRODUCED: 6214 (carburettor version); 11,669 (fuel-injection version).
ENGINE: Bore 93.5mm, stroke 85.5mm, capacity 2347cc, maximum power 115bhp (DIN) at 5500rpm with Weber 34 DM TR 35 twin-choke carburettor or 128bhp (DIN) at 4800rpm with Bosch L-Jetronic fuel-injection.
TRANSMISSION: All-synchromesh manual gearbox, four-speed on carburettor version, five-speed on fuel-injection version. Three-speed C-matic semi-automatic transmission with floor-mounted selector optional until 09/1980; ZF three-speed automatic transmission with floor-mounted selector optional thereafter; final drive ratio: 3.49:1; gear ratios: first 2.48:1; second 1.48:1; third 1.00:1.
TYRES: 185 HR 14 at front and rear.
STEERING: Rack and pinion, with 'Varipower' hydraulic power assistance as standard.
DIMENSIONS: Length: 4.92m (193.6in); width: 1.73m (68.1in); height: 1.38m (54.3in); wheelbase: 3.095m (121.9in).
KERB WEIGHT: 1475kg (3252lb).

CX 2400 GTi (Series 1)

KEY DIFFERENCES
ENGINE: Bore 93.5mm, stroke 85.5mm, capacity 2347cc, maximum power 128bhp (DIN) at 4800rpm, Bosch L-Jetronic fuel-injection.
TRANSMISSION: Five-speed manual gearbox with synchromesh on all gears. Final drive ratio: 4.77:1; gear ratios: first 3.17:1; second 1.83:1; third 1.25:1; fourth 0.94:1; fifth 0.73:1.
TYRES: 185 HR 14 at front and rear.
STEERING: Rack and pinion, with 'Varipower' hydraulic power assistance as standard.
KERB WEIGHT: 1364kg (3007lb).
CAPACITIES: Fuel: 68l (15.0gal); boot: 0.475m³ (16.8ft³).

CX 2200D and 2500D (Series 1)

KEY DIFFERENCES
NUMBER PRODUCED: 57,949 saloons + 11,104 estates (2200: 1975-1978); 199,229 saloons + 4,617 limousines + 48,855 estates (2500: 1977-1984).
ENGINE: Water-cooled, four-cylinder diesel. Bore 90mm (2500: 93mm), stroke 85.5mm (2500D: 92mm), capacity 2175cc (2500D: 2500cc), maximum power 66bhp (DIN) at 4500rpm (2500D: 75bhp (DIN) at 4250rpm), Roto-Diesel injection.
TRANSMISSION: Four-speed manual gearbox

with synchromesh on all gears (2500: five-speed optional from 1978). Final drive ratio: 4.77:1 (2500: 4.54:1); gear ratios first 3.17:1; second 1.83:1; third 1.13:1; fourth 0.8:1; (2500D five-speed: first 3.17:1; second 1.83:1; third 1.25:1; fourth 0.94:1; fifth 0.73:1).
TYRES: Front: 185 SR 14; rear: 175 SR 14 (2500: 185 SR 14).
STEERING: Rack and pinion, with 'Varipower' hydraulic power assistance as standard.
KERB WEIGHT: 1330kg/2932lb (2500: 1342kg/2965lb).

By 1979, the results of Peugeot's takeover of Citroën were starting to take effect. The company's old 2-litre petrol engine was replaced by a modern, light-alloy OHC unit of similar capacity (1995cc), which had been developed jointly with Renault and was also fitted to the Renault 20 and Peugeot 505. The 2000 models were renamed the CX Reflex and CX Athena (after the Greek goddess of wisdom), the latter having more luxurious trim, together with power steering and a five-speed gearbox as standard. The new engine was quieter and more flexible, as well as delivering better fuel economy. This 'Douvrin' engine could not be enlarged to 2.4 litres, however, so Citroën's 2347cc engine soldiered on.

In November 1979, the CX Limousine was launched: this combined the long-wheelbase Prestige body with the 2500cc diesel engine.

Inside, it was finished similarly to the Athena. The following year, a five-speed gearbox became standard equipment on both the 2500 Diesel and the Athena, while the 2347cc petrol engine received a boost in power. In September 1980, a conventional torque converter automatic gearbox, supplied by ZF, replaced the optional C-matic on the Pallas and Prestige. This necessitated widening the front track, a change made on all models. The next two years saw various minor changes to the cars' standard and optional equipment. In 1981, for instance, cruise control became an option on the Pallas, Prestige and GTi, while the rustproofing applied by the factory was progressively improved. For 1982, the front wheelarches were enlarged, allowing Michelin TRX tyres to be fitted: these were standard on the GTi and an option on the fuel-injected Pallas and Prestige models.

In July 1982, the range was restructured. The Reflex name was dropped, with the result that the petrol model became simply the CX 20 and its diesel counterpart the CX 25 D. The Athena name was replaced by a new TR trim level, bringing the CX 20 TRE (with a five-speed manual transmission) in line with Citroën's approach to model names at the time. Not in the UK, however, where the traditional 'Pallas' name was retained in preference to 'TRE.' The centre console was redesigned at this point, and the spherical ashtray was no more.

1983 model year CX 20 TRE at La Ferté-Vidame. (Courtesy Citroën Communication)/ Marc Desmoulins)

CX 20 Reflex and Athena (1979-1982)

KEY DIFFERENCES
ENGINE: Water-cooled, four-cylinder petrol, transversely mounted, SOHC design. Bore 88mm, stroke 82mm, capacity 1995cc, maximum power 106bhp (DIN) at 5500rpm, Weber 34 DM TR 46/250 carburettor.
TRANSMISSION: Five-speed manual gearbox with synchromesh on all gears. Final drive ratio: 4.54:1; gear ratios: first 3.17:1; second 1.83:1; third 1.25:1; fourth 0.94:1; fifth 0.73:1.
TYRES: Front: 185 HR 14; rear: 175 HR 14.
STEERING: Rack and pinion, with 'Varipower' hydraulic power assistance standard on Athena, optional on Reflex.
DIMENSIONS: Turning circle (between kerbs): 11.7m (38.4ft).
KERB WEIGHT: 1220kg (2690lb).
CAPACITIES: Fuel: 68l (15.0gal); boot: 0.458m³ (16.2ft³).

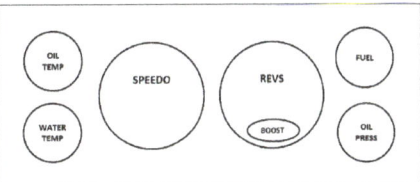

Dashboard for pre-facelift CX GTi Turbo. (Courtesy Citroën Communication)

1983 saw some important changes to both the diesel and petrol engines. In April, a turbocharger was fitted to the 2500cc diesel (initially without an intercooler), raising its power output to 95bhp. This was available in two trim levels, as the CX 25 RD Turbo or TRD Turbo; in the UK, the latter was known as the DTR Turbo. The turbodiesel engine was also fitted to the long-wheelbase limousine model. In July 1983, the capacity of the 2347cc fuel-injected petrol engine was raised one more time, to 2500cc, full electronic ignition was added and power went up to 138bhp (DIN).

Even this, however, left Citroën hard placed to compete with its six-cylinder rivals in the executive saloon category. In October 1984, the company therefore launched the CX 25 GTi Turbo: as with the turbodiesel, there was no intercooler to start with, but power rose to 168bhp (DIN), and there were significant gains in torque and flexibility. It should be noted, however, that Citroën never offered the turbocharged petrol engine with automatic transmission. In March 1985, the CX 25 GTi Turbo became the first French car to have ABS as an option. The GTi Turbos from the first year of production are now highly sought after, as they combined the pre-facelift exterior with the later dashboard with a full complement of round dials. The non-turbocharged GTi continued, with the option of automatic transmission, and a new RI model with simpler equipment was added to the range until 1988.

Series 1 CX GTi Turbo. (Courtesy Citroën Communication)

CX 25 GTi Turbo (1984-1989)

KEY DIFFERENCES
NUMBER PRODUCED: 12,912 (Series 1 and 2)
ENGINE: Water-cooled, four-cylinder petrol, transversely mounted, OHV layout. Bore 93mm, stroke 92mm, capacity 2500cc, maximum power 168bhp (DIN) at 5000rpm, Bosch L-Jetronic fuel-injection and Garrett T03 turbocharger.
TRANSMISSION: Front-wheel drive, five-speed manual gearbox with synchromesh on all gears. Final drive ratio: 4.21:1; gear ratios: first 3.17:1; second 1.83:1; third 1.21:1; fourth 0.88:1; fifth 0.67:1.
BRAKES: ABS optional from 1985.
TYRES: Michelin TRX 210/55 VR 390.
STEERING: Rack and pinion, with 'Varipower' hydraulic power assistance as standard.
KERB WEIGHT: 1385kg (3053lb).

In April 1984, to maintain interest in the model, Citroën introduced the limited-edition CX Leader: mechanically, this was based on the five-speed CX 20, but had distinctive metallic silver paint with darker lower body panels, plastic wheel trims, a rear spoiler, tinted glass and tartan cloth seats. 700 were built in the first year, but it proved an attractive package and nearly 10,000 cars were sold until 1988. Citroën applied the same recipe to the BX and the Visa a few months later. The Leader was the main limited-edition CX, but Citroën sold a small number of 'Sélection' special edition cars in 1988: these were based on the 20 RE saloon, with a rear spoiler and specific wheel trims and decals.

COLOURS (All Series 1 models 1975-1984): Beige Colorado, Gris Squale, Gris Neptune, Gris Perlé, Beige Nevada, Gris Espadon, Beige Opale, Beige Gazelle, Gris Vulcain, Gris Largentière, Beige Vanneau, Blanc Meije, Noir, Sable Cendré, Sable Doré, Rouge Masséna, Brun Scarabée, Rouge Soleil, Orange Mandarine, Brun Vésuve, Rouge Dragon, Brun Roquebrune, Rouge de Garance, Vert Guérande, Vert Iroise, Vert Papyrus, Vert Dryades, Vert Tamaris, Vert Tamarin, Vert Chartreuse, Vert Amazonie, Bleu Nuit, Bleu Lagune, Bleu Delta, Bleu Régate, Bleu Centaurée, Bleu Océan, Bleu Polaire, Bleu Argenté.

Leader special edition, here in post-facelift guise.

CX saloon: Series 2

By the summer of 1985, the CX was over ten years old and faced fresh competition from Renault's new 25, ironically, also designed by Robert Opron. Citroën therefore launched the facelifted Series 2 CX for the 1986 model year. Updated by Carl Olsen, it can immediately be identified by its plastic bumpers, protective rubbing strips and profiled wing mirrors (which would be reused by several other manufacturers).

Inside, it had a completely restyled dashboard with round instruments and a sloping centre console, but still had minor control pods to each side of the instrument binnacle. Central locking and a one-touch driver's window were among the new features added. A new CX 22 TRS saloon joined the facelifted range, with a 2165cc carburettor version of the 'Douvrin' four-cylinder engine, slotting in above the 20 RE. ABS was now fitted as standard to the CX 25 GTi Turbo and the newly introduced CX 25 Prestige Turbo, which had the engine from the GTi Turbo installed in the long-wheelbase Prestige body.

In September 1986, an air-to-air intercooler was at last fitted to the CX 25 GTi Turbo and CX 25 Prestige Turbo, both renamed Turbo 2. Maximum power remained unchanged, but the revised model had higher gearing for better economy. A few months later, in February 1987, the turbodiesel also received an intercooler: it developed 120bhp and was for a while the quickest production diesel car in the world.

That year, the CX 25 GTi served as a testbed for the 'Hydractive' suspension which would be introduced on the forthcoming XM. About a dozen so-called 'REGAMO' prototypes ('REG' for 'Régulation' and 'AMO' for 'Amortisseur' (shock absorber)) were built, of which at least one has survived. These were the last significant changes to the CX saloon before the XM arrived in May 1989 to take its place and production of the CX saloon came to an end at Aulnay-sous-Bois. Altogether, 883,995 saloons and 29,380 long-wheelbase Prestige and Limousine models were built.

Post-facelift models: GTi Automatic, Prestige Turbo and GTi Turbo.

Interior of facelifted GTi Turbo. (Courtesy Citroën Communication)

CX 22 TRS (1985-1989)

KEY DIFFERENCES
ENGINE: Water-cooled, four-cylinder petrol, transversely mounted, SOHC design. Bore 88mm, stroke 89mm, capacity 2165cc, maximum power 115bhp (DIN) at 5600rpm, Weber 34 DM TR 110/100 carburettor.
TRANSMISSION: Five-speed manual gearbox with synchromesh on all gears. Final drive ratio: 4.36:1; gear ratios: first 3.17:1; second 1.83:1; third 1.25:1; fourth 0.94:1; fifth 0.73:1.
TYRES: Front: 195/70 R 14; rear: 185/70 R 14.
STEERING: Rack and pinion, with 'Varipower' hydraulic power assistance as standard.
DIMENSIONS: Length: 4.65m (183.1in); width: 1.77m (69.7in); height: 1.36m (53.5in); wheelbase: 2.845m (112in); turning circle (between kerbs): 10.8m (35.5ft).
KERB WEIGHT: 1275kg (2811lb).
CAPACITIES: Fuel: 68l (15.0gal); boot: 0.458m^3 (16.2ft^3).

CX 25 DTR Turbo (1983-1987) and Turbo 2 (1987-1989)

KEY DIFFERENCES
NUMBER PRODUCED: 55,741 saloons + 2089 limousines + 11,241 estates.
ENGINE: Water-cooled, four-cylinder diesel. Bore 93mm, stroke 92mm, capacity 2500cc, maximum power 95bhp (DIN) at 3700rpm (Turbo 2: 120bhp (DIN) at 3900rpm), Roto-Diesel injection (Turbo 2: Lucas injection), Garrett T03 turbocharger (Turbo 2: Garrett T025).
TRANSMISSION: Front-wheel drive, five-speed manual gearbox with synchromesh on all gears. Final drive ratio: 3.81:1 (Turbo 2: 3.69:1); gear ratios: first 3.17:1; second 1.83:1; third 1.21:1; fourth 0.88:1; fifth 0.67:1 (Turbo 2: first 3.42:1; second 1.95:1; third 1.25:1; fourth 0.88:1; fifth 0.67:1).
TYRES: Michelin TRX 190/60 HR 390.
STEERING: Rack and pinion, with 'Varipower' hydraulic power assistance as standard.
KERB WEIGHT: 1385kg/3053lb (Turbo 2: 1360kg/2998lb).
CAPACITIES: Fuel: 68l (15.0gal); boot: 0.458m^3 (16.2ft^3).

COLOURS (All Series 2 models 1985-1989): Beige Sphinx, Brun Maya, Cassis Nacré, Rouge Florentin, Rouge Delage, Rouge Vallelunga, Bleu Iris, Bleu Memphis, Bleu Navy, Bleu Romantique, Bleu Magnétic, Vert Cali, Gris Renard, Blanc Crémant, Gris Météor, Beige Impala.

CX estate: Series 1 and 2

Launched in October 1975, the estate version of the CX shared its long-wheelbase chassis with the Prestige saloon and had a raised roof over the rear seats and luggage compartment. The very first estates built had no side rubbing strips, but these soon became standard. A Familiale version, with seven seats in three rows, was added 12 months after the regular estate.

The estates subsequently followed the general evolution of the saloons in terms of their equipment and engines. For 1981, Citroën introduced a revised range of Reflex-badged estates: the 2000 Reflex Safari, CX 2000 Reflex Familiale, 2400 Reflex Safari and 2400 Reflex Familiale. The turbocharged petrol engine was never installed in the estate body, but two fully equipped, high-performance versions were introduced in July 1983: the CX 25 TRI estate with the 138bhp (DIN) fuel-injected 2.5-litre petrol engine, and the TRD Turbo estate (known, like the saloon, as DTR Turbo in the UK) with the turbodiesel engine.

In March 1984, Citroën launched the tax-saving CX 20 and CX 25 D Entreprise models. As was customary, the rear doors were welded shut and only the front seats were fitted, leaving a long, fully lined load bay behind them.

Following the major facelift of the CX range in July 1985, the estates continued with the 2.5-litre turbodiesel, the 2-litre, or the fuel-injected 2.5-litre petrol engines. Five-seat models (still called 'Safari' in the UK) or seven-seat Familiale models were available. The fuel-injected 2.5-litre petrol engine came with a choice of five-speed manual transmission or a Borg Warner three-speed auto.

For much of its career, the special rapid intervention group (GIGN) of the French Gendarmerie Nationale was a regular user of the CX estates, always fitted with the most powerful fuel-injected engines available and

Pre-facelift estates; the silver car is a high-performance 25 TRI. (Courtesy Citroën Communication)

with lower gearing for quicker acceleration. Like the DS before it, the CX estate was also favoured by camera crews, including those of the BBC.

When the CX saloon was replaced by the XM in 1989, the French coachbuilder Heuliez took over production of the CX estate for a further two years until the XM estate was introduced. The UK model range in 1990 comprised the 22 TGE Safari, 25 TGI Safari and 25 TGD Safari Turbo Diesel.

NUMBER PRODUCED: Series 1 and 2: 128,185 (estate); 900 (Entreprise).
DIMENSIONS: Length: 4.95m (194.9in); width: 1.73m (68.2in); height: 1.47m (57.6in); wheelbase: 3.095m (121.9in); turning circle (between kerbs): 12.5m (41.0ft).

Post-facelift car has larger, plastic bumpers

Citroën Cars 1934 to 1986 – A Pictorial History

Ex-Gendarmerie estate for sale at auction.

KERB WEIGHT: 1320-1462kg (2910-3223lb), depending on engines and equipment.
CAPACITIES: Fuel: 68l (15.0gal); boot (all seats folded): 2.1m^3 (74.2ft^3).

Special bodies

The CX saloon's fastback styling naturally lent itself to a hatchback configuration, and demand for this layout increased from Citroën's customers. The company's official response came with the five-door XM in 1989, but some small-scale conversions were carried out on the CX, notably by Caruna and Beutler in Switzerland.

The estate served as the basis for the officially sanctioned CX ambulance, presented in September 1976. Construction of this followed a somewhat convoluted route: Citroën sent a standard estate to the coachbuilder Carrier in Argenteuil, who stripped out the rear bench seat and fittings and installed a new floor panel on the left with sliding rails to accommodate a stretcher with telescopic legs. But the customer then had to turn to specialists such as Baboulin, Collet, Heuliez or Petit to have the vehicle fully kitted out for service as an ambulance. Heuliez, for example, offered two different types of rear compartment with different roof heights and tailgate arrangements. If it was too late for an

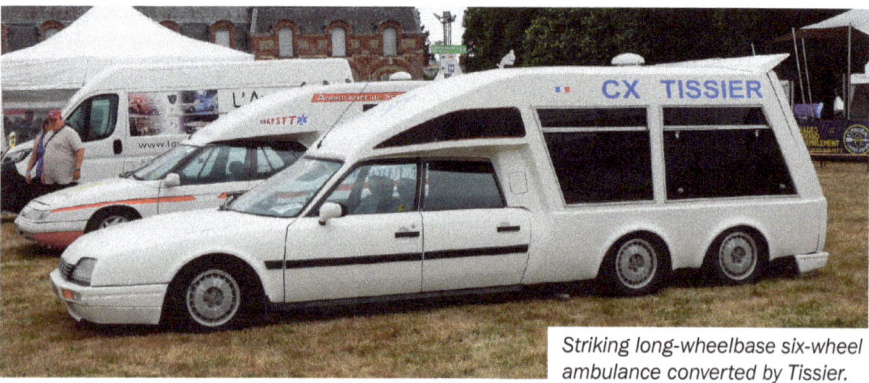

Striking long-wheelbase six-wheel ambulance converted by Tissier.

Chapron-bodied CX 2400 Prestige Landaulet from 1981.

The CX Orphée convertible. (Courtesy Osenat)

ambulance, Heuliez also offered a CX-based hearse.

The French specialist Tissier developed a number of six-wheel versions of the CX with twin rear axles and an extended fibreglass body. Some of these were used for rapid deliveries of newspapers across France, others as ambulances or people carriers. Nowadays, some Tissier six-wheelers have also been converted into historic race car transporters.

What is sadly missing from the history of the CX, however, are the fantastic convertible models that Chapron built for the DS. After Henri Chapron's death, his company built a handful of landaulets in 1981 with either foldback or plexiglass roofs, which saw service at various royal weddings in Europe.

Chapron also prepared a quotation for a French engineer and Citroën enthusiast, Guy Deslandes, to produce a CX convertible, but the price was too high for him. Deslandes therefore decided to build his own convertible, based on a CX 2400 GTi, with lengthened front doors and specially made side windows. Christened the CX Orphée, just one prototype and four complete cars were produced in 1983-1984. Deslandes also built a single CX coupé, the Avrilly, in 1984.

SM

The origins of the SM go back to 1961, when Citroën began work on 'Projet S,' a two-door sports version of the DS. In the end, the only two-door DS saloons produced were a small number of special cars built for rallying, and Citroën followed a fresh and much more ambitious path when it bought Maserati in 1968. The SM (familiarly known as 'Sa Majesté' – Her Majesty) was at the heart of this relationship: a joint venture to produce a brand-new GT which would combine a glorious Italian V6 engine and the French company's remarkable hydropneumatic systems. It was intended to be Citroën's flagship and a showcase for French technology; at much the same time, in March 1969, Concorde made its first test flight. Although Citroën only sold the SM as a two-door coupé, a number of special bodies were created by independent coachbuilders.

The SM was unveiled at the Geneva Motor Show in March 1970. The fastback body was styled by Robert Opron, who was also responsible for the GS, launched the same year, and the CX; it had a Kamm tail and was remarkably efficient aerodynamically. The bonnet was made from high-grade aluminium and the exterior trim was stainless steel rather than chrome. For the first time on a mass-produced model, the windscreen was bonded. Despite its hatchback design and greater length than the DS, the rear seats were fixed and it was strictly a 2+2. The interior was as distinctive as the exterior, with oval dials for the main gauges behind the company's customary single-spoke steering wheel. The wheel could be adjusted for both height and reach, another first on a European production car.

Citroën provided the car's hydraulic systems, which reached new levels of sophistication,

Concorde provides a backdrop to Chapron-bodied SM Opéra and Mylord. (Courtesy Citroën Communication)

with power brakes (now using discs all round) and 'Diravi' (for 'Direction à Rappel Asservi') variable-assistance power steering. The steering, also known as 'Varipower' in English, took some getting used to: it was very quick (with only two turns from lock-to-lock) and had powerful self-centring. Where the DS had two headlamps on each side, the European-spec SM had three under a glass cover, all self-levelling and with the innermost pair linked to the car's steering, as on the DS. Like all Citroën's cars since the Traction Avant, the SM naturally had front-wheel drive.

The engine was an all-new quad-cam V6 designed by Giulio Alfieri, and was based on the 4.2-litre V8 used in the Indy, with two fewer cylinders. It was a compact, aluminium unit, weighing 140kg (309lb) and mounted behind the front axle to improve the car's weight distribution. Its capacity was limited to 2.7 litres to avoid the additional French tax ('super-vignette') levied on cars with engines of over 2.8 litres. The SM launched with a five-speed manual gearbox taken from the DS, but with a conventional, floor-mounted gearlever in a chrome gate. The same engine was also fitted to the Ligier JS2 sports car, while the Maserati Merak used a larger 3-litre version of the engine, as well as hydraulically powered brakes and pop-up headlamps. Meraks built before 1975 even had the same dashboard as the SM.

The SM was widely praised for its dynamic qualities. In 1971, on its first outing in competition, it came first in Group 4 in the demanding Rallye du Maroc, following on from the successes of the DS in Morocco in 1969 and 1970. Just before the SM went out of production in 1975, Citroën produced a short-wheelbase car for competition, nicknamed 'the breadvan'; only a handful were produced, but by then the SM's career was virtually over.

At launch, the SM was the fastest front-wheel drive car on sale, but above all, it offered a unique blend of style, comfort and handling. Its many famous owners included the musicians Bill Wyman of the Rolling Stones and Adam Clayton of U2, President Leonid Brezhnev of the Soviet Union, the Shah of Iran and Idi Amin of Uganda (who allegedly had seven!). Another notable customer was the French Gendarmerie Nationale, which took delivery of five SMs in 1972 to patrol the country's autoroutes.

The SM's crowded engine bay. Note green spheres for hydraulic system.

Rare competition version of the SM.

Gendarmerie Nationale SM on the A6 autoroute south of Paris. (Courtesy Citroën Communication/Georges Guyot)

SM coupé

The SM went on sale in France in September 1970. A single version was offered: a two-door coupé with manual transmission. The cars had cloth upholstery as standard, but black or natural leather upholstery was an option. Air-conditioning, tinted glass and fog lamps were further options, as was a radio, mounted vertically next to the handbrake.

Steel wheels with stainless steel trims were fitted as standard, but the SM could be specified with Michelin reinforced resin wheels, which had originally been developed for rallying and were very strong, while a few cars can sometimes be seen with starfish-style alloy wheels.

From 1970-1972, the V6 engine was fitted with three twin-choke Weber carburettors, but in September 1972 this setup was replaced by Bosch D-Jetronic electronic fuel-injection. The new engine produced slightly more power but was primarily developed to meet the more stringent emissions regulations coming into force in Europe. Citroën already had experience with fuel-injection, which was introduced on the DS 21 IE in 1969, and the new version was intended to be more reliable and deliver improved fuel consumption. Cars with the fuel-injected engine had an 'Injection électronique' badge on the tailgate.

In July 1973, for the 1974 model year, the company introduced a new version of the SM with a three-speed automatic transmission supplied by Borg Warner. This was mated to a three-litre version of the V6 engine, as installed in the Maserati Merak, and reverted to the use of three Weber carburettors. An estimated 600

SM at La Ferté-Vidame in 2019. (Courtesy Citroën Communication)

Promotional photos for the SM at its launch. (Courtesy Citroën Communication)/Robert Delpire)

The luxurious interior of the SM could be specified with leather or cloth upholstery. (Courtesy Citroën Communication)

cars were also fitted with the 3-litre engine and manual transmission. The introduction of the automatic model was prompted, above all, by the requirements of the USA and Canadian markets: with their traditionally strong demand for two-door 'personal luxury cars,' these were the main export territories Citroën targeted.

Although the engine was down on torque compared with the local V8s, reviewers were

Reinforced resin wheels on the white 'Mylord' and starfish alloys on the blue coupé.

enthusiastic and the SM was even voted 'Car of the Year' by *Motor Trend* magazine in 1972. US legislation required that all cars had round, sealed-beam headlamps on fixed mounts, so SMs sold in North America lost the distinctive frontal treatment of the European models. Unfortunately, this was not the end of Citroën's problems: for 1974, the US authorities mandated a fixed front bumper height, something the SM's variable-height suspension made impossible. The SM was therefore withdrawn from sale in North America after 2400 cars had been sold in 1972 and 1973. 100 of the cars delivered in the US had an electric sliding sunroof engineered by ASC. The final batch of cars intended for the USA and Canada in 1974 was sold in Japan.

A handful of right-hand drive conversions were carried out in the UK (by Middleton Motors) and Australia (by Chapel Engineering in Victoria), but all SMs left the factory with left-hand drive and the majority of cars were sold in Europe. Apart from the engine and transmission developments described above, there were few other changes for the remainder of the SM's career. In 1974, Citroën's historic factory at the Quai de Javel in Paris closed, and production of the SM was taken over by Ligier at its site in Vichy.

By then, however, the writing was on the wall for the SM. The market for all high-performance cars had been hit by the oil crisis in 1973 and the economic recession that followed. The SM was a complex car to maintain, and Citroën's traditional dealers were unused to keeping highly-strung Italian engines like the SM's in tune. Production of the SM fell from 5032 cars in 1971 and 3992 cars in 1972 to just 294 cars in 1974. With Citroën facing bankruptcy once again, Peugeot stepped in at the end of 1974 to save the company. Citroën's new owner took the decision to sell Maserati in May 1975; the Italian state took control that summer and Alejandro de Tomaso was appointed the new CEO.

The SM's short career and limited production compared with many of the cars presented in this book make it all the more collectable today. It was left to the far more conventional Peugeot 604 saloon to take over the mantle of the PSA Group's flagship. Much of the SM's technology, including its pioneering 'Varipower' steering would live on,

North American model with round headlamps. (Courtesy Citroën Communication)

Reconstruction of SM V8.

however, in the CX, introduced in 1974.

All the production SMs were fitted with naturally aspirated V6 engines, but a couple of special versions are worthy of note. One SM was fitted in period with Maserati's V8 engine and used for development work on the 1974 Maserati Quattroporte II, although this ultimately went into production with the V6 engine from the Merak SS. Several years later, the American specialist Jerry Hathaway of SM World in Los Angeles developed a twin-turbo V6 version of the SM, and in 1987 set a speed record of 202mph (325km/h) on the Bonneville Salt Flats in America.

In France, the best-known tuner associated with the SM was Georges Regembeau, who had already worked his magic on the Traction Avant 15 Six. For the SM, he developed a 2.4-litre four-cylinder turbodiesel engine for better economy, but also worked on the V6 petrol engine to improve its reliability. His changes to the V6 resulted in a massive increase in maximum power (to 240bhp with carburettors and 250bhp with fuel-injection), while a six-speed manual gearbox ensured more relaxed high-speed cruising. These Regembeau-modified V6-engined cars are now highly sought after by collectors.

NUMBER PRODUCED: 12,920
PRICE AT LAUNCH: 50,000FF
ENGINE: Water-cooled, 90-degree V6 petrol, twin OHC per bank. Bore 87mm, stroke 75mm, capacity 2670cc, maximum power 170bhp (DIN) at 5500rpm (with fuel-injection: 178bhp (DIN) at 5500rpm), three twin-choke Weber 42 DCNF carburettors (1970-1972), then Bosch D-Jetronic electronic fuel-injection (1972-1975).
3.0 automatic: Bore 91.6mm, stroke 75mm, capacity 2965cc, maximum power 180bhp (DIN) at 5500rpm, three twin-choke Weber 42 DCNF carburettors.
TRANSMISSION: Front-wheel drive, five-speed manual gearbox with synchromesh on all gears, floor-mounted gearlever. Final drive ratio: 4.375:1; gear ratios: first 2.93:1; second 1.94:1; third 1.32:1; fourth 0.97:1; fifth 0.81:1 (with fuel-injection: 0.76:1).
3.0 automatic: Three-speed Borg Warner automatic transmission with floor-mounted selector.

Citroën Cars 1934 to 1986 – A Pictorial History

BRAKES: Front: discs (mounted inboard); rear: discs. Hydraulic servo control and dual circuits.
TYRES: 195/70 VR 15 (with fuel-injection: 205/70 VR 15).
SUSPENSION: Fully independent self-levelling hydropneumatic, with front wishbones and rear trailing arms. Anti-roll bars at front and rear, anti-dive and anti-squat geometry.
STEERING: Rack and pinion, with speed-related variable power assistance and automatic self-centring ('Diravi'/'Varipower').
DIMENSIONS: Length: 4.89m (192.5in); width: 1.84m (72.4in); height: 1.32m (52.0in); wheelbase: 2.95m (116.2in); turning circle (between kerbs): 10.9m (35.7ft).
KERB WEIGHT: 1450kg (3197lb); with fuel-injection: 1490kg (3285lb).
CAPACITIES: Fuel: 90l (19.8gal); boot: 0.25m³ (9.0ft³).
COLOURS:
1970 only Blanc Cygne.
1971 only Feuille Dorée, Rouge de Rio (or Rouge Brasilia), Bleu Platine.
1971-1972 Sable Métallisé, Vert des Tropiques.
1971-1973 Gris Nacré.
1971-1975 Blanc Meije, Noir.
1972 only Rouge de Grenade.
1972-1973 Bleu d'Orient.
1972-1975 Brun Scarabée, Vert Argenté.
1973 only Bleu de Brégançon.
1973-1975 Beige Tholonet, Or de Simiane.
1974-1975 Gris Largentière, Brun de Roquebrune, Bleu Delta.

Nearly all SMs were sold with single-colour bodywork, but a small number of cars had duotone paintwork, combining white, red or grey main panels and a black or grey roof.

Gear change layout of the SM.

Special bodies

In 1971, a year after the launch of the coupé, two French coachbuilders presented their proposals for open versions of the SM. Heuliez's 'Espace' prototype, of which two were built, was a pillarless targa-top convertible with elegant slatted blinds extending over the front seats. Henri Chapron's 'Mylord,' on the other hand, had a conventional soft top without a rollover bar. Chapron presented his car

Heuliez's 'Espace' prototype with targa-style roof arrangement.

SM

Close-up of Heuliez's 'Espace' prototype with the roof blinds opened up.

Below: Open and closed views of Chapron's 'Mylord' conversion of the SM.

69

at the 1971 Paris Motor Show and hoped that Citroën would sell it, as it had the DS 'Décapotable Usine,' but Citroën declined, on the grounds that the conversion would compromise the strength of the body. Just five 'Mylord' models were built from 1971-1973.

A year after the 'Mylord,' Chapron presented a second special-bodied SM at the 1972 Paris Motor Show: the four-door, three-box 'Opéra' saloon. The wheelbase of this was extended by 29cm (11.4in) and it had an overall length of 5.19m (204.3in). Seven cars were produced from 1972-1974.

The 'Opéra' served as the basis for the most famous special-bodied SM, the 'Présidentielle,' a four-door landaulet with a long rear overhang. It measured 5.60m (220.5in) overall and weighed in at 1890kg (4167lb). The French President Georges Pompidou ordered two Présidentielle models for ceremonial use in 1971, and they were inaugurated the following year, when the British monarch Queen Elizabeth II made a

Chapron's four-door 'Opéra' saloon.

Queen Elizabeth II and President Pompidou in the SM Présidentielle. (Courtesy Citroën Communication/Jean Peyrinet)

The interior of the Présidentielle.

state visit to France. They remained in service until 2007.

The Italian coachbuilder Frua produced an attractive coupé concept based on the SM in 1972, but it never went into production.

On an altogether different note, in 1977 the French coachbuilder Tissier built a one-off ten-wheeled breakdown truck, with a load platform behind the coupé's cabin, which has recently been restored.

Frua-bodied SM.

Citroën Cars 1934 to 1986 – A Pictorial History

2CV and derivatives

Slow and ugly, but one of the best-loved Citroëns of all time, the 2CV has a huge following among enthusiasts throughout the world. When it was conceived in the 1930s, however, its future cult status was far from the mind of Pierre Boulanger, Citroën's chairman. His aim was to bring motorised transport to the many French people unable to afford a car, including the farmers still using horse-drawn carts. It was intended to be cheap to buy and to run, but to offer space for four and a ride that could cope with farm tracks and ploughed fields as well as paved roads. Even its roll-back fabric sunroof had a practical purpose, to accommodate oversized items.

Development of what was known as the TPV (for 'Toute Petite Voiture') began before the Second World War under the direction of André Lefèbvre, who had already been responsible for the Traction Avant. It was originally planned to have aluminium body panels and a water-cooled 700cc engine. A pilot run of 250 cars was built in 1939, but plans to launch the car were abandoned with the outbreak of war. Most of the cars already built were destroyed, but a few were hidden, and five prototypes are believed to survive. After the war, Citroën revised its plans: the body was restyled by Flaminio Bertoni, using flat steel panels that were cheaper to produce, and the water-cooled engine made way for an air-cooled flat-twin designed by Walter Becchia, mated from the outset to a four-speed gearbox. Inside, the seats were redesigned, using tubular steel frames with rubber bands stretched across them.

Original 2CV prototype from 1939. (Courtesy Citroën Communication)

Named the 2CV – in reference to its French fiscal horsepower rating – the new Citroën made its début at the Paris Motor Show in October 1948, with full-scale production starting in July 1949. Despite its unfamiliar appearance and minimalist design, it quickly became a massive success, with a waiting list of up to three years. The 2CV was the first mass-produced small car with front-wheel drive, and introduced several major innovations: its 375cc air-cooled engine, all-round independent suspension (interconnected from front to rear), and even a brand-new radial tyre from Michelin, Citroën's owner. The body was built on an H-frame platform chassis with a tubular framework and thin but light steel panels bolted to it. Its simple engine was slow and noisy, initially producing only 9bhp. But the 'Tin Snail' had low fuel consumption and was easy and cheap to maintain. To prevent the engine from running too cool in winter, owners could cover part of the front grille with a muff (originally made from canvas, later from plastic) to limit the flow of air.

The 2CV – and its many derivatives built on

2CVs lined up at the Citromuseum in Castellane.

the same A-Series platform – went on to enjoy a remarkably long career, with the last 2CV finally coming off the lines in 1990. Altogether, more than nine million A-Series cars and light vans (including the Ami range described in the next chapter) were built, in plants across Europe and South America and even in Asia and Africa. Some of these countries went so far as to develop their own models, such as the three-box Citroneta in Chile or the Méhari Ranger station wagon in Uruguay.

2CV

Throughout its 42-year career, the core A-Series model was the four-door 2CV saloon, always fitted with a full-length opening roof. The first phase in its career encompasses the period from 1948-1960 and includes all the Type A cars fitted with the original 375cc engine, which was dropped for the 1960 model year. These early cars had a so-called 'ripple bonnet' with integrated side panels, a four-light body (ie, with no windows in the rear quarter panels) and 'suicide' front doors. Until 1957, the fabric roof on French-built cars extended down to the rear bumper to serve as a boot lid, as fabric was cheaper than steel after the war. The speedometer was mounted on the driver's door pillar and the windscreen wipers driven off it.

Over time, the spartan 2CV gradually gained some additional equipment and more powerful

2CVs coming down the production line. (Courtesy Citroën Communication)

An early 'ripple-bonnet' 2CV on the streets of Tours.

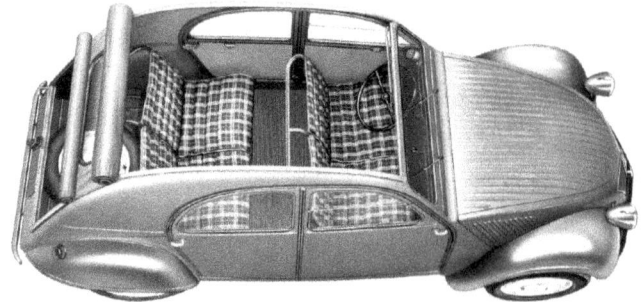

(Courtesy Citroën Communication)

engines. In 1953, an ignition lock and lockable driver's door were added; the paintwork was now a lighter shade of grey and the seats were upholstered in tartan cloth. Two years later, for the 1955 model year, Citroën responded to its customers' demands for more power and introduced the AZ model with a 425cc engine developing 12bhp (SAE) and a centrifugal clutch. For 1957, striped upholstery replaced the tartan cloth. At the same time, the AZL ('L' for 'Luxe,' or Luxury) was added to the range: this had the same mechanical specification as the AZ, but with improved equipment including a demister and an enlarged rear window. For 1958, the AZLP ('P' signifying 'Porte de malle' or boot lid) was introduced, with a lockable

The original dashboard. (Courtesy Citroën Communication)

Period publicity photo shows rear-hinged door. (Courtesy Citroën Communication)

2CV and derivatives

metal boot lid for the first time on French-built cars. An extended boot lid, to increase the luggage capacity, could also be bought as an accessory. In 1959, the heater and demister were improved. For the 1960 model year, blue was offered as an alternative colour, with yellow soon added as well, and a removable Radioën transistor radio became an option. 380mm diameter wheels replaced the original 400mm items, and the 375cc Type A model finally went out of production.

Unlikely though it may seem, the 2CV competed in motorsport during the 1950s, a Type A model even taking part in the Tour de France automobile in 1951. Jean Dagonet, from northern France, went a good deal further, initially modifying the standard engine, suspension and transmission, before creating his own bodies with a lowered roofline. For his part, Pierre Barbot created a low-slung two-door roadster on a shortened 2CV chassis in 1953.

Three types of boot covering (L-R): metal lid on French car; original fabric covering; metal lid on Belgian-built car.

Accessory boot lid extension.

Left: Dagonet 2CV.

Below: Barbot 2CV.

Citroën Cars 1934 to 1986 – A Pictorial History

2CV TYPE A and AZ (1949-1960)

NUMBER PRODUCED: 3,867,932 (all versions, 1948-1990).
ENGINE: Air-cooled, petrol, with two horizontally opposed cylinders (flat-twin), OHV layout. Bore 62mm (AZ: 66mm), stroke 62mm, capacity 375cc (AZ: 425cc), maximum power 9bhp (SAE) at 3500rpm (AZ: 12bhp (SAE) at 3500rpm), Solex single-choke carburettor.
TRANSMISSION: Front-wheel drive, four-speed manual gearbox, dashboard-mounted gearlever, AZ: centrifugal 'Trafficlutch.' Final drive ratio: 3.875:1; gear ratios: first 6.69:1; second 3.24:1; third 1.94:1; fourth 1.48:1.
BRAKES: Front: inboard drums; rear: drums.
TYRES: 125 X 400 Michelin Pilote (135 X 380 from 09/1959).
SUSPENSION: Fully independent but interconnected front to rear with longitudinal coil springs, inertia and friction dampers.
STEERING: Rack and pinion.
DIMENSIONS: Length: 3.78m (148.8in); width: 1.48m (58.3in); height: 1.60m (63.0in); wheelbase: 2.40m (94.5in); turning circle (between kerbs): 10.5m (34.4ft).
KERB WEIGHT: 495kg (1091lb).
CAPACITIES: Fuel: 20l (4.4gal); boot: 0.21m³ (7.5ft³).
COLOURS:
At launch Dark Grey only.
From 1953 Light Grey.
From 1960 Blue (Bleu Glacier) added.

December 1960 marked the start of the second stage in the 2CV's career: cars built after this date can be easily identified by their new, smoother bonnet with five lengthwise ribs. The 1962 model year saw the addition of the 2CV 'ENAC Mixte,' with a single-piece lifting tailgate and a removable rear seat, giving a flat load floor of 1.15m (45.3in). The spare wheel was also moved under the bonnet, to free up additional load space. This model was available until the end of the 1967 model year. At the end of 1962, output of the 425cc engine went up to 13.5bhp (SAE); an electric wiper motor was fitted and there was a new trapezoidal instrument panel in front of the driver with the speedometer and a fuel gauge, replacing the measuring rod of the original cars.

In February 1963, Citroën launched the AZA model, based on the AZLP but with the letter 'A' denoting 'Améliorée' (improved). This was soon succeeded by the further enhanced AZAM, as Citroën responded to competition from the more modern and better equipped Renault 4. The AZAM sported chrome bumper overriders and headlamp surrounds, additional brightwork on the bonnet and more comfortable seats taken from the Ami 6. Power increased to a heady 18bhp (SAE).

For the 1965 model year, the front doors became front-hinged, while a year later French-built 2CVs gained a new six-light body with additional side windows in the rear quarter panels. (The six-light body had in fact

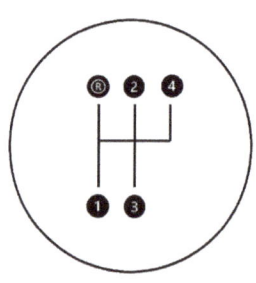

2CV gear change layout.

Front doors remained rear-hinged until 1965.

2CV and derivatives

Citroën still promoted the 2CV to rural customers. (Courtesy Citroën Communication)

been introduced on the 2CV AZL cars built in Belgium as early as 1957). 1966 saw some additional engineering changes: constant velocity driveshafts were fitted (as standard or an option, depending on the model) and the friction dampers at the rear were replaced by telescopic hydraulic shock absorbers. In 1967, the biggest change was the introduction of a new dashboard (carried over from the Ami 6), initially on the short-lived top-of-the-range 2CV AZAM Export model; this design would continue in use until the end of the 2CV's career. During 1968 and 1969 there were only minor changes; the AZAM model was dropped in 1969 after the Dyane was launched.

By the start of 1970, despite the catchy marketing slogan 'an umbrella on four wheels,' the 2CV's sales were in decline. Citroën therefore restructured the 2CV range, with two models offered in most markets, powered by a new generation of higher revving engines. The 2CV4 had a 435cc engine producing 26bhp at 6750rpm, while the 2CV6 – technically now a 3CV model in tax terms – was equipped with a 602cc engine based on that used in the Ami 6, developing 33bhp and greater torque than the 435cc unit. 12-volt electrics with an alternator replaced the original 6-volt system and new taillight clusters were fitted. Bright new colours (red, green, blue and yellow) gave

Six-light body and front-hinged doors were only fitted to French-built cars from 1965.

Citroën Cars 1934 to 1986 – A Pictorial History

The new dashboard design introduced in 1967. (Courtesy Citroën Communication)

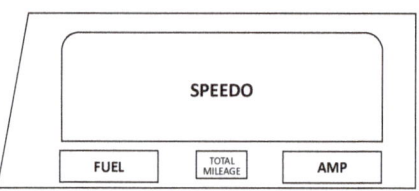

the cars a fresher look. A padded single-spoke steering wheel was fitted on the 2CV6, and three-point front seatbelts became standard. The oil crisis of 1973 provided a welcome fillip to the 2CV's sales, and, in 1974, 2CV production reached its highest ever level, with 163,143 cars built. In October 1974, rectangular headlamps were fitted. At the same time, the UK reintroduced the 2CV6: having just joined the EEC the UK was able to avoid the crippling import duties of the past.

With a new-found appeal among younger,

(Courtesy Citroën Communication/Georges Guyot)

economy-minded customers, the 2CV was set to embark on the third and final stage in its career. This would be characterised by some final technical changes, efforts to improve its safety, and the introduction of numerous limited editions to boost its appeal.

First though, in July 1975, Citroën expanded the range with the 2CV Spécial, a stripped-down model based on the 2CV4. The new model reverted to the old four-light body with round headlamps and a hood that could only be opened from the outside. It had slimmer bumpers without overriders, and no hubcaps. Inside, it was just as spartan, with vinyl upholstery and a single-piece front bench seat. The trapezoidal metal instrument panel and two-spoke plastic steering wheel fitted in the 1960s were reused, while the ashtray, interior light and passenger sunvisor were all dispensed with. Even the door cards were simplified and had exposed catches. The first cars for the French market were all finished in 'Jaune Cédrat' (yellow) with a black roof; cars sold in Switzerland were red. In autumn 1978, Citroën repented somewhat: the third side window made its return and the range of colours was progressively extended. Production of the 2CV4 ended in September 1978, but the 2CV Spécial kept the 435cc engine until mid-1979, when the 602cc engine became standard on all models. For a single year (1981-82) the company offered the 2CV6 Spécial E with a standard centrifugal clutch. The 2CV4 Spécial was never sold in the UK, but in 1982 the 2CV6 Spécial went on sale as the cheapest new car on the British market.

The 602cc engine was revised in 1976 to meet the latest emissions regulations, and again in 1979 when it was fitted with a twin-choke carburettor: it now produced 29bhp (DIN) but had improved torque and fuel economy. In 1979, the 'regular' 2CV6 was renamed the 2CV6 Club and received separate front seats trimmed in a striped fabric similar to that used in the Dyane. For 1982, the 2CV became the last A-Series model to receive front disc brakes: these were easier to replace than the drums, as well as providing greater stopping power. As European safety legislation evolved, the 2CV gained inertia-reel seatbelts in the front and three-point static belts in the rear.

2CV and derivatives

Original 2CV Spécial. (Courtesy Citroën Communication)

Sales of the 2CV in the UK actually peaked in 1986, when 7520 cars were sold, but the writing was on the wall for the now hopelessly outdated model, which had no chance of meeting the planned safety and emissions regulations. In 1988, production came to an end at the old and inefficient factory in Levallois-Perret, on the outskirts of Paris, and was transferred to Mangualde in Portugal for two more years. The very last 2CV, a grey Charleston, was built on 27 July 1990.

Later six-light Spécial. (Courtesy Citroën Communication)

The Spécial reverted to the older dashboard design. (Courtesy Citroën Communication)

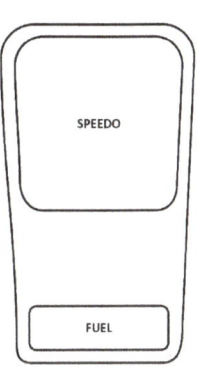

Citroën Cars 1934 to 1986 – A Pictorial History

Rectangular headlamps for the 2CV6 and 2CV6 Club. (Courtesy Citroën Communication/Malard)

Striped seats on 2CV6 Club from 1979 onwards. (Courtesy Citroën Communication/ Malard)

2CV6 (1979-1990)

KEY DIFFERENCES
ENGINE: Bore 74mm, stroke 70mm, capacity 602cc, maximum power 29bhp (DIN) at 5750rpm, Solex 26/35 twin-choke carburettor.
TRANSMISSION: Four-speed manual gearbox. Final drive ratio: 4.125:1; gear ratios: first 5.20:1; second 2.66:1; third 1.79:1; fourth 1.32:1.
BRAKES: Front: inboard drums (inboard discs from 1982); rear: drums.
TYRES: 125 X 15 Michelin X.
SUSPENSION: Fully independent but interconnected front to rear with longitudinal coil springs, hydraulic shock absorbers at front and rear.
DIMENSIONS: Length: 3.83m (150.8in); width: 1.48m (58.3in); height: 1.60m (63.0in); wheelbase: 2.40m (94.5in); turning circle (between kerbs): 9.9m (32.5ft).
KERB WEIGHT: 560kg (1235lb).
CAPACITIES: Fuel: 25l (5.5gal); boot: 0.27m^3 (9.4ft^3).
COLOURS:
1970-1983 Gris Cormoran, Beige Colorado, Beige Nevada, Beige Gazelle, Beige Vanneau,

2CV and derivatives

Ivoire Borély, Beige Albatros, Blanc Meije, Beige Erable, Blanc Cygne, Noir, Jaune Primevère, Orange Ténéré, Jaune Cédrat, Jaune Mimosa, Cuivre Indien, Jaune Hélios (Charleston), Rouge Masséna, Rouge Rio, Rouge Soleil, Rouge Géranium, Mandarine, Rouge de Castille, Rouge Delage (Charleston), Rouge Vallelunga, Vert Palmeraie, Vert Tuileries, Vert Bambou, Vert Jade, Bleu Thasos, Bleu Camargue, Bleu Lagune, Bleu Pétrel, Bleu Myosotis, Bleu Azurite.
1984-1990 Jaune Rialto, Rouge Delage (Charleston), Rouge Vallelunga, Bleu Nuit, Bleu Céleste, Bleu des Tropiques, Gris Cormoran, Gris Nocturne (Charleston), Blanc Meije, Noir, Beige Colorado, Bleu Lagune (from 10/1983), Bleu des Tropiques.

Limited editions

In the final years of the 2CV's life, Citroën produced several limited editions to bolster its sales. Mechanically, these were identical to the standard 2CV4 and 2CV6 models but had distinctive colour schemes. Serge Gevin, who worked in Citroën's design department from 1976–2015, was responsible for nearly all of them, as well as the Dyane Caban and Méhari Azur.

The first limited edition sold in France was the Spot, of which 1800 were built in 1976. This was based on the 2CV4 but had the dashboard and rectangular headlamps from the 2CV6. It had orange and white bodywork and a jauntily striped sunshade.

The Spot was followed in 1980 by the Charleston, based on the 2CV6 Club. Three Art Déco-style colour schemes were offered: maroon (Rouge Delage) and black (the most popular combination), yellow (Jaune Hélios) and black, or two-tone grey. It proved so successful that in July 1981 it became a permanent model at the top of the 2CV range, with standard-fit front disc brakes. Cars from the first year of production had round headlamps with painted surrounds and houndstooth check cloth upholstery, but cars from 1981 onwards had chrome-plated headlamp surrounds and quilted grey upholstery. In 2008, Citroën applied the same colour scheme to a limited edition of the C3 Pluriel to mark the 2CV's 60th anniversary.

In 1981, Roger Moore drove a yellow 2CV6 – stealthily upgraded with the 1015cc flat-four engine from the GS – in the James Bond film *For Your Eyes Only*. This was the basis for the 2CV 007, which was also painted yellow with an '007' logo on the front doors and fake

The 2CV Spot. (Courtesy Citroën Communication)

Citroën Cars 1934 to 1986 – A Pictorial History

Yellow and black: the rarest colour combination for the Charleston. (Courtesy Citroën Communication)

Below: The Charleston was most commonly seen in maroon and black; two-tone grey also offered.

bullet hole decals. Sadly, it was fitted with the standard 602cc engine. 700 examples were produced.

Two years later, Citroën sponsored a French crew in the America's Cup, and in March 1983 it brought out a commemorative special edition of the 2CV known, like the boat, as the France 3. Based on the 2CV6 Spécial, it was finished in white (Blanc Meije) with distinctive blue graphics and special upholstery to match the exterior. 2000 cars were built in 1983, followed by a second run of 2000 in 1984.

James Bond's most unlikely car?

2CV and derivatives

The same model was sold in England as the Beachcomber and in Germany as the Transat (French for 'deckchair').

Next up, in 1985, was the Dolly, based on the 2CV6 Spécial but with a range of bright, two-tone colour schemes: initially grey and white, grey and red and grey and yellow. Later, red and white, green and white, dark blue and

2CV France 3. (Courtesy Citroën Communication)

2CV Dolly.

83

cream, and maroon and cream (nicknamed 'plums and custard' in the UK) were added. Like the Charleston, this proved a big hit, especially in the UK, where it became the best-selling version. Altogether, 5000 cars were built in 1985-1986.

The final special edition of the 2CV in France was the Cocorico (French for 'cock-a-doodle-doo'), the rooster being one of the country's national emblems. It was finished in the colours of the French flag: blue, white and red. 1000 cars were produced in 1986.

Citroën's distributors outside France produced a few special editions of their own:
- In Spain, 300 examples of the 2CV Marcatelo were produced in 1982 to mark the country's hosting of the World Cup;
- In Switzerland, the 1984 Week-end edition was based on the 2CV6 Spécial;
- In Italy, Citroën offered two limited editions based on the 2CV6 Spécial with duotone paintwork and special decals: the Soleil (yellow and white) and the Scala (red and white);
- In Belgium and Luxembourg, the 2CV Perrier sold in 1988-1989 had white paintwork with special graphics, wheel trims made to look like bottle caps and a coolbox inside the car;
- Finally, three countries offered limited editions with Bamboo Green paintwork and special logos: in 1985, the 'I fly bleifrei' (ie on unleaded fuel) in Germany, and in 1987 the 'Sauss-Ente' in Switzerland and the 2CV Bamboo in the UK.

Although not sold to the public, a couple of other special 2CVs should be mentioned. The first of these was the 2CV Basket of 1977, of which two examples were created for display in Citroën's showroom on the Champs-Elysées.

In 2008, as a tribute to the 2CV's 60th birthday, Citroën presented a special model at the Paris Motor Show, produced in association with the couturier Hermès. Based on a 1989 2CV Spécial, this was finished in brown with elegant leather trim inside.

Cocorico!

Special graphics for the Italian-market Soleil. (Courtesy Citroën Communication)

Interior of the 60th anniversary Hermès commemorative model. (Courtesy Citroën Communication/Patrick Legros/Hermès)

2CV and derivatives

4x4 Sahara

One other special version of the 2CV deserves a mention of its own: the remarkable 4x4 model, produced by Citroën to meet the needs of oil exploration firms in North Africa and first presented in 1958. Originally known as the 4x4 Sahara, the 'Sahara' tag was dropped in 1962.

Not only did this have four-wheel drive, but also twin 425cc engines (one at each end of the vehicle), developing a combined power output of 26bhp (SAE), and two four-speed gearboxes. It had a pair of 15-litre (3.3gal) fuel tanks, with fillers routed through the front doors, and wider, 155-section Michelin X radial tyres. Unsurprisingly, the 4x4 model cost twice as much as a standard 2CV. It was able to climb gradients of more than 40%, but the second engine – in what would have been the boot – limited its load capacity. Altogether 694 cars were produced, essentially from 1960-1967, but with just one car built in 1971. Much later, from 1982 onwards, the French specialist Voisin offered a four-wheel drive conversion of the standard front-engined 2CV.

Dyane

(Courtesy Citroën Communication)

Door-mounted fuel fillers were among the distinctive changes to the 2CV 4x4.

Second engine in what would have been the boot. (Courtesy Citroën Communication)

By 1964, the 2CV had been on sale for 15 years and was facing tough competition from the Renault 4, with its practical hatchback body and more powerful four-cylinder engines. Citroën therefore began work on the AY project, led by Louis Bonier at Panhard, which Citroën acquired in 1965. The company initially intended that the 2CV would remain on sale as a cheaper, entry-level model alongside the new car rather than being immediately replaced. The Dyane continued to use the 2CV chassis and engine, but the body – still with a full-length opening roof – was completely new. Like the Renault 4, it was a hatchback; the concave door panels and headlamps integrated into the front wings gave it a distinctive and more modern appearance. Inside, there was a new design of dashboard incorporating fresh air vents.

The Dyane was launched in France in August 1967, in basic Luxe and better equipped Confort versions. The latter had hubcaps as standard, cloth upholstery and moulded plastic door panels with map pockets; the spare wheel was located under the bonnet to free up space in the boot. A Commerciale model for business users was also offered (until 1974). Initially, the Dyane had a four-light body, just like the early 2CVs;

85

(Both photos courtesy Citroën Communication)

the 425cc engine was also carried over from the older car, but developed 21bhp (SAE) rather than 18bhp in this application, thanks to a different carburettor. The centrifugal 'Trafficlutch' offered on the 2CV was available as an option (until 1982). The Dyane was still criticised, however, for its lack of power, and in January 1968, Citroën added the Dyane 6 with the 602cc engine from the Ami 6, further uprating it to 33bhp (SAE) in September that year. The original AYA model continued alongside the Dyane 6 (which was rated in France at 3CV), but in March 1968, it was replaced by the Dyane 4 with a new 435cc engine producing 26bhp (SAE). It was only at the end of 1969, however, that a third side window was fitted.

During the 1970s, the basic formula of the Dyane remained unchanged, but there was a series of incremental improvements. As on the 2CV, brighter colours became available, and from 1972 the doorhandles were mounted below, rather than above the belt line. In 1974, there were new brushed aluminium model badges, and the Dyane enjoyed record sales (with 126,854 ced a new style of plastic front grille, and in 1976, the Dyane 4 was dropped.

To boost its appeal, in 1977 Citroën produced 1500 examples of the Dyane Caban limited edition. This had dark blue

Early Dyane 6 with four-light body.

2CV and derivatives

(Courtesy Citroën Communication)

d'Azur: this was finished in white (Blanc Alaska) with bright blue decals and hood. It is easy to think of the Dyane as a failure, insolently outlived by the 2CV, but altogether 1.4 million examples were built.

The Dyane enjoyed particular success in Spain and Portugal, where the car maker had factories. In 1975, Citroën added a specific model for the Portuguese market, the Nazaré, with tartan seats and wind-down front windows, as fitted to the Acadiane van. Wind-down front windows, as well as sliding rear windows, were also fitted to cars sold in Spain (the Dyane normally had sliding front windows and fixed rear windows). Citroën Hispania sold two unique limited editions in 1981:

- The Edelweiss (750 cars) had metallic blue paint, black bumpers, GSA-style wheel trims and a luggage rack mounted on the tailgate;
- The Capra (600 cars) had yellow paint with black trim and the same GSA-style wheels as the Edelweiss.

The Dyane was also built in Belgium, in present-day Slovenia (then part of Yugoslavia) by Tomos and then Cimos, and in Iran, where its rear wheelarches were cut away and it was renamed the Jyane 602.

paintwork with a white hood and graphics, and houndstooth cloth upholstery. It was sold in France and in export markets including Germany, Switzerland, the UK and the Benelux. Also in 1977, for one year only, Citroën made the Dyane available with metallic beige (Beige Opale) paint and special cloth upholstery.

Several safety features were added during the 1970s and early 1980s, including a driver's door mirror and standard front seatbelts. In the rear, seatbelt anchorage points were fitted. The biggest change in terms of the car's active safety, however, came in 1978, with the adoption of front disc brakes.

In September 1978, there was a new design of vertically striped seat upholstery (the author's own car from this period had a particularly snazzy combination of beige, dark brown and orange!). There would be few other major changes until the end of the Dyane's career in 1983. Just before the end of production, in 1982-1983, Citroën offered another limited edition in the UK, the Côte

Dyane 6 (1978-1983)

NUMBER PRODUCED: 1,443,583 (all versions, 1967-1983).
ENGINE: Air-cooled, two-cylinder (flat-twin) petrol, OHV layout. Bore 74mm, stroke 70mm, capacity 602cc, maximum power 32bhp (DIN) at 5750rpm, Solex 26/32 twin-choke carburettor.
TRANSMISSION: Front-wheel drive, four-speed manual gearbox, dashboard-mounted gearlever. Final drive ratio: 3.875:1.
BRAKES: Front: inboard discs; rear: drums.
TYRES: 125 X 15 Michelin X.
SUSPENSION: Fully independent but interconnected front to rear with longitudinal coil springs, hydraulic shock absorbers at front and rear.
STEERING: Rack and pinion.
DIMENSIONS: Length: 3.87m (152.4in); width: 1.50m (59.1in); height: 1.54m (60.6in); wheelbase: 2.40m (94.5in); turning circle (between kerbs): 10.6m (34.8ft).
KERB WEIGHT: 600kg (1323lb).
CAPACITIES: Fuel: 25l (5.5gal); boot: 0.34m³/0.98dm³ (12.1ft³/34.6ft³).

Méhari

In May 1968, Citroën struck out in a quite different direction, when it presented the Méhari – named after a camel used by the Berbers – at Deauville. After rejecting an earlier concept from Heuliez, Citroën accepted a proposal from SEAB. For the first time, it was clearly intended to be a leisure-oriented, fun derivative of the 2CV, and it soon became a regular sight in French beach resorts. But it was also a practical vehicle: the French Army bought 7064 of them and it even spawned a capable four-wheel drive model. All the cars had left-hand drive and it was never officially sold in the UK.

Mechanically, the Méhari was closely based on the Dyane 6, but it was the first mass-produced car to feature injection-moulded ABS plastic bodywork (made from just 13 components), riveted to a tubular frame and mounted on a shortened AK 350 van chassis. It had removable doors, a folding rear seat and a basic roof canopy; a plastic hardtop was available as an accessory. The colour was incorporated into the ABS plastic during manufacture and the range of colours offered – all named after desert regions – was limited.

During a career spanning nearly 20 years, the Méhari changed relatively little. In 1969, the power output of the 602cc flat-twin increased slightly, from 26bhp (DIN) to 29bhp. The following year, a two-seat model was added so that sales tax could be reclaimed on it in France, and there was a new front grille and lights. In 1969-1970, the Méhari was sold in the US, with changes made to the front panel, boot lid, lights and electrical equipment to meet local requirements. But the venture was short-lived, with only 214 cars sold.

From 1971, the windscreen could be folded down and hydraulic rear shock absorbers were fitted. Hydraulic front shock absorbers followed in 1975. In 1976, as on the 2CV, power fell to 26bhp (DIN) as the engine was revised to meet new emissions regulations. For the 1978 model year, it was the turn of the Méhari to receive front disc brakes

Original advertisement for the Méhari. (Courtesy Citroën Communication)

2CV and derivatives

Early Méhari with original design of front grille. (Courtesy Citroën Communication)

with a dual-circuit braking system. The grille design was again revised. For 1979, power went back up to 29bhp (DIN) when a twin-choke carburettor was fitted. A more modern dashboard, taken from the LNA, replaced the original panel from the 2CV.

In 1983, Citroën introduced a limited edition of the Méhari known as the Azur. This had a unique two-tone colour scheme in white and dark blue, with matching striped seats and a folding hood which was easier to erect. 700 cars were built in 1983, and it proved so popular that it became a regular model in 1984. A further limited edition was sold in Spain and Portugal in 1983: built at Mangualde in Portugal, the Plage (beach) had yellow bodywork and white wheels.

The Méhari was built in Belgium, Argentina and Yugoslavia as well as in France, Spain and Portugal. Production came to an end in 1987 after 144,953 cars had left the lines, but the Méhari was not forgotten: it served as the inspiration for an electric car, the e-Méhari, in 2016 and even an 'Art Car' by the French fashion designer Jean-Charles de Castelbajac in 2019.

Updated dashboard from 1979. (Courtesy Citroën Communication)

COLOURS:
1968-1975 Rouge Hopi.
1968-1977 Beige Kalahari.
1968-1987 Vert Montana.
1969-1987 Orange Kirghiz.

1976-1979 Vert Tibesti.
1978-1987 Beige Hoggar.
1980-1987 Jaune Atacama.

Special blue and white paint job for the Méhari Azur.

Méhari 4x4

In May 1979, Citroën launched a four-wheel drive version of the Méhari. It had disc brakes all round and could be recognised by its bonnet-mounted spare wheel and specific dashboard with round Jaeger instruments, including a rev counter. Unlike the 2CV Sahara, however, the Méhari 4x4 only had a single engine (installed at the front), so it was lacking in power. This, and its high price (twice that of the 2WD version), hampered sales and production ceased in 1983.
NUMBER PRODUCED: 1213.
ENGINE: Air-cooled, two-cylinder (flat-twin) petrol, OHV layout. Bore 74mm, stroke 70mm, capacity 602cc, maximum power 29bhp (DIN) at 5750rpm, Solex 26/35 twin-choke carburettor.
TRANSMISSION: Four-wheel drive, four-speed manual gearbox with reduction gearing on three gears, dashboard-mounted gearlevers, lockable differential. Final drive ratio: 3.875:1.
BRAKES: Front: inboard discs; rear: discs.
TYRES: 135 X 15 (M+S).
SUSPENSION: Fully independent but interconnected front to rear with longitudinal coil springs, hydraulic shock absorbers at front and rear.
STEERING: Rack and pinion.
DIMENSIONS: Length: 3.52m (138.6in); width: 1.53m (60.2in); height: 1.63m (64.4in); wheelbase: 2.40m (94.5in); turning circle (between kerbs): 10.8m (35.4ft).
KERB WEIGHT: 720kg/1587lb (2WD: 525kg/1157lb).
CAPACITIES: Fuel: 25l (5.5gal).

Promotional photos for the Méhari 4x4. (Courtesy Citroën Communication)

Vans
2CV Fourgonnette

Two years after the launch of the 2CV saloon, Citroën presented the Fourgonnette (van) version at the 1950 Paris Motor Show. This was officially known as the AU, with 'U' signifying 'Utilitaire.' At first, it had the same 375cc engine as the Type A saloon, but with wider 135-section tyres and a lower final drive ratio (4.43:1) to cope with the loads it would carry. For all that, its top speed was only 60km/h (37mph).

In 1955, Citroën fitted the 425cc engine and it became the AZU 250, in reference to its 250kg (551lb) payload. The van kept the conventional manual gearbox with a clutch pedal rather than the AZ saloon's centrifugal clutch. In 1958, a demister was fitted and in 1961 the new five-rib bonnet made its appearance. For 1963, the 425cc engine was uprated to 18bhp (SAE) and the corrugated upper side panels were replaced by smooth panels to make signwriting easier. The doors were now front-hinged. At this point, Citroën added a new model, the AK 350, with a longer wheelbase and reinforced chassis to compete with the Renault 4 van; it was fitted with the 602cc engine from the Ami 6 and could carry a maximum load of 350kg (772lb).

In July 1970, Citroën went a stage further when it introduced the AKS 400: this was mechanically identical to the AK 350, but had a higher roof and 400kg (882lb) payload. In 1975, both the AZU 250 and AKS 400 received the plastic grille as fitted to the 2CV saloons and – for just one year – rectangular headlamps. Side windows in the rear returned for 1977 after being dropped for a time for tax reasons.

PRODUCTION NUMBERS: (all models) 1,246,299.
DIMENSIONS: Length: 3.60m/141.7in (AU/AZU); 3.80m/149.6in (AK/AKS); width: 1.50m (59.1in); height: 1.72m/67.7in (AU/AZU/AK); 1.83m/72.2in (AKS).
CAPACITIES: load space: 1.88m³/66.4ft³ (AU/AZU/AK); 2.1m³/74.2ft³ (AKS).

The evolution of the 2CV Fourgonnette over three decades. (Middle photograph courtesy Citroën Communication, lower courtesy Citroën Communication/Georges Guyot)

Load compartment of a 1975 AKS 400. (Courtesy Citroën Communication/Georges Guyot)

Acadiane

In March 1978, the 2CV-based AZU and AKS vans were replaced by the new Acadiane model. As its name – a combination of AK and Dyane – suggested, this was based on the Dyane and shared its frontal styling and dashboard. Unlike the Dyane, however, wind-down windows in the front doors were fitted from the outset, as were inertia-reel front seatbelts. The load space, with a raised roofline, was comparable to the AKS 400, but it had an increased payload of 480kg (1058lb) and its improved aerodynamics gave it a slightly higher top speed. In France and the Benelux, a 'Mixte' version with sliding rear windows and a removable rear bench seat was also offered, a forerunner to the modern Berlingo.

All Acadianes had the 602cc engine, as well as front disc brakes. The suspension was to a heavier-duty specification, but was no longer interconnected from front to rear. The most important mechanical development came in July 1980, when Citroën introduced a version of the Acadiane running exclusively on LPG, with a 63-litre (13.9gal) tank mounted behind the front seats. Performance was similar to the

(Courtesy Jeremy Clarke)

petrol model. In practice, however, few LPG-equipped vehicles were sold.

The other changes to the Acadiane were less significant. In July 1979, a folding front passenger seat was offered as an option, and in October that year a load-sensitive rear brake limiter was fitted. In 1983 a laminated windscreen became standard, and in 1984 the service intervals were extended. Production continued until July 1987, by which time the more modern, Visa-based C15 was

(Courtesy Citroën Communication)

2CV and derivatives

well established. Nearly all the Acadianes were built at Vigo in Spain, where the model was known locally as the Dyane 400. From 1981-1985, Cimos built about 2200 Dak vans and 900 Geri pickup trucks based on the Acadiane in Yugoslavia.

NUMBER PRODUCED: 253,393.
ENGINE: Air-cooled, two-cylinder (flat-twin) petrol, OHV layout. Bore 74mm, stroke 70mm, capacity 602cc, maximum power 31bhp (DIN) at 5750rpm, Solex twin-choke carburettor.
TRANSMISSION: Front-wheel drive, four-speed manual gearbox, dashboard-mounted gearlever. Final drive ratio: 3.875:1.
BRAKES: Front: inboard discs; rear: drums.
TYRES: 135 X 15.
SUSPENSION: Fully independent, with hydraulic shock absorbers at front and rear.
STEERING: Rack and pinion.
DIMENSIONS: Length: 4.03m (158.7in); width: 1.53m (60.2in); height: 1.83m (71.8in); wheelbase: 2.54m (99.8in); turning circle (between kerbs): 11.2m (36.7ft).
KERB WEIGHT: 685kg (1510lb).
CAPACITIES: Fuel: 25l (5.5gal); load space: 2.27m^3 (80.2ft^3).
COLOURS:
1978 Blanc Alaska, Bleu Myosotis, Beige Gazelle.
1979 Blanc Alaska, Bleu Myosotis, Beige Nevada.
1980-1981 Blanc Alaska, Bleu Azurite, Beige Nevada.
1982-1983 Blanc Alaska, Bleu Lagune, Beige Colorado.
1984 Blanc Meije, Bleu Camargue, Beige Impala.
1985 Blanc Meije, Bleu Uzès, Beige Impala.
1986 Blanc Meije, Bleu Uzès, Beige Atlas.
1987 Blanc Meije, Bleu Céleste, Beige Atlas.

FAF

In some ways resembling a metal-bodied Méhari, the FAF – built from 1977-1981 – was aimed at a very different market. FAF stood for 'Facile à Fabriquer, Facile à Financer' (Easy to Build, Easy to Finance) and the FAF was conceived as a tough and practical utility vehicle for use in developing countries, not unlike the independently built 'Baby Brousse' from Ivory Coast in the 1960s. The FAF was based mechanically on the 2CV, but used folded steel panels in a range of body styles: van, pickup, saloon and estate. It had similar overall dimensions to the Méhari.

At the end of 1978, Citroën presented a

Military version of the FAF.

Citroën Cars 1934 to 1986 – A Pictorial History

1983 'Croisière Jeune' special edition of the FAF.

four-wheel drive version of the FAF at the Dakar Fair in Senegal. Powered by the 652cc flat-twin from the Visa, it was intended primarily for military use in Africa, although a civilian version was also available. An estimated 1786 FAFs were built, in Portugal, Africa and Indonesia, but only ten or so had four-wheel drive.

UK-built cars

Production of the 2CV could only begin at Slough in 1953, as the inboard-mounted front drum brakes fitted to the early cars were illegal under British vehicle regulations before then. As with the Traction Avant, Citroën was able to avoid paying import

Slough-built 2CVs had a metal boot lid long before the models produced in France did.

2CV and derivatives

Bonnet badge unique to UK-built cars.

duties by assembling the 2CV locally, but its price was still too high to be competitive and sales were poor.

Cars built in the UK had a metal boot lid long before those in France and different bumpers, as well as hinged rear windows (on the French cars, these were always fixed), a special 'Front Drive' bonnet badge and semaphore-type indicators to meet local requirements. The first cars built in the UK had the 375cc engine, but the 425cc engine was fitted after it had been introduced on the Type AZ in France. Altogether, 673 2CVs were produced at Slough from 1953-1960, of which 340 were exported to Australia. To meet the sometimes harsher conditions there and in South Africa, improved air cleaners were fitted to all the cars built in the UK.

The UK factory also built a special pickup version of the van during the 1950s, but only 66 civilian-spec vehicles were produced. In 1959, however, the British government placed an additional order for 65 2CV pickups for deployment with the Royal Marines. The Marines needed tough, reliable vehicles that were light enough to be dropped from helicopters.

Bijou

In 1959, Citroën introduced a unique model in the UK, the Bijou. Intended to be more stylish and conventional than the regular 2CV, it was built on the A-Series platform, but had a two-door coupé body. Made from fibreglass, it was designed by Peter Kirwan-Jones, better known for his work on the original Lotus Elite. Inside, it had a single-spoke steering wheel (like the DS) and a more conventional dashboard than the 2CV. The rear seat could be folded down to carry longer items.

The body was surprisingly ungainly, however, with the rear of the car standing 15cm (6in) higher than the front. Although

Citroën Cars 1934 to 1986 – A Pictorial History

it was quite efficient aerodynamically, the Bijou was 100kg (220lb) heavier than the 2CV, and the standard 425cc AZ engine was too low-powered to give the car adequate performance. The Bijou was launched at the 1959 London Motor Show, but all eyes were on BMC's new Mini and it struggled to make a mark. Although Citroën reportedly lost money on each car it built, the Bijou was also too expensive and suffered from poor build quality. In the end, just over 200 cars were built at Slough from 1959-1964.

NUMBER PRODUCED: 207–212 (estimates vary).
PRICE AT LAUNCH: £674
ENGINE: Air-cooled flat-twin petrol, OHV layout. Bore 66mm, stroke 62mm, capacity 425cc, maximum power 12bhp (SAE) at 4000rpm, single-choke Solex carburettor.
TRANSMISSION: Front-wheel drive, four-speed manual gearbox with centrifugal clutch. Final drive ratio: 3.875:1; gear ratios: first 6.75:1; second 3.25:1; third 1.93:1; fourth 1.47:1.
BRAKES: Front: inboard-mounted drums; rear: drums.
TYRES: 135 x 380 Michelin radial.
SUSPENSION: Fully independent but interconnected front to rear with longitudinal coil springs, inertia and friction dampers; front: leading arms; rear: trailing arms.
STEERING: Rack and pinion.
DIMENSIONS: Length: 3.96m (155.9in); width: 1.55m (61.0in); height: 1.17m (46.1in); wheelbase: 2.39m (94.1in); turning circle (between kerbs): 10.5m (34.3ft).
KERB WEIGHT: 603kg (1330lb).
CAPACITIES: Fuel: 20l (4.4gal).
COLOURS: Coral, Daffodil, Dove Grey, Sherwood Green.

Ami and M35

As France's middle classes began to prosper during the 1950s, Citroën increasingly needed another model to bridge the gap between the basic 2CV and the much more expensive ID. It therefore started work on 'Projet MI' (for 'Modèle Intermédiaire'). This would lead to the introduction of the Ami 6 in April 1961, shortly ahead of the Renault 4. Pierre Bercot, Citroën's managing director, stipulated that it should have a traditional three-box design with a large boot and room for five passengers, but with a length of under 4m (just over 13ft). In truth, however, it was closer to the 2CV than the ID, as it used the same platform as the 2CV and had a larger (602cc) version of its two-cylinder engine, developing 22bhp at launch. The first cars were built in Paris, but in September

On the production line at Rennes-la-Janais. (Courtesy Citroën Communication)

The Ami 6 was revealed to the press in April 1961. (Courtesy Citroën Communication)

(Courtesy Citroën Communication)

1960 most production transferred to a new, purpose-built factory at Rennes-la-Janais in Brittany. Some cars were also produced in Spain, Belgium, Yugoslavia and Argentina.

In 1964 Citroën introduced an estate version of the Ami 6, which proved very popular, and in 1966 the Ami 6 became France's best-selling car. In 1969 both models were replaced by the Ami 8, which remained in production until 1979. It was joined by the Ami Super from 1973-1976: this used the four-cylinder engine from the GS and took the Ami further upmarket. The Ami 8 also served as the basis for the remarkable M35 prototype, Citroën's first foray into rotary power. Altogether, over 1.8 million Amis were built.

Ami 6

The Ami 6 was the last Citroën to be designed by Flaminio Bertoni, who reportedly considered it his favourite. It certainly had distinctive styling, with its pagoda-like roof and central dip in the bonnet, a design change brought about by the French authorities' concerns about the headlamp height. Above all, however, Bertoni's design stood out on account of its reverse-raked rear window (like that of the Ford Anglia 105E), which was intended to prevent rain or snow accumulating on the screen. The roof was initially made from fibreglass and riveted to the body. The Ami had sliding front windows, but the rear windows were fixed until autumn 1961. The large rectangular headlamps were specially developed by Cibié for greater efficiency, but Export models (sold in the US from 1963) had four round headlamps, which were also fitted to the Ami 6 Club from October 1967. At first, only four colours were available, but the palette was progressively extended.

Inside, the Ami 6 had more luxurious seats than the 2CV, while some fittings were inspired by the DS, including the door handles, single-spoke steering wheel and some minor controls. In its promotional materials for the new model, Citroën was at pains to stress that it was altogether new and much more upmarket than the 2CV.

In September 1962, the 'standard' Ami 6 was renamed the Confort and fitted with an adjustable front bench seat. It was joined by an entry-level model, the Tourisme: this had simpler bumpers without a central bar and no

(Courtesy Citroën Communication/Georges Guyot)

(Courtesy Citroën Communication)

(Courtesy Citroën Communication)

hubcaps, as well as a fixed front bench and more basic interior trim. The company probably went a step too far, however, and it was not a success. In 1963, a number of changes were made to the engine and electrics, while the friction dampers were replaced by Boge hydraulic shock absorbers. Further incremental improvements were made during 1964 and a centrifugal clutch became an option. The biggest changes, however, came that autumn, for the 1965 model year, with a more powerful 25.5bhp (SAE) engine and the addition of a five-door estate model.

Designed by Henri Dargent, Bertoni's assistant, and Robert Opron, the estate had more conventional styling than the saloon and boasted a capacious luggage compartment and 320kg (705lb) payload. Three versions were offered in France: the four-seat Break, five-seat Familiale and – following the company's tradition – the ambulance. The estate was a huge success, quickly outselling the saloon and accounting for 80% of Ami sales in France in 1967.

During 1966 and 1967, Citroën continued to improve the saloon and estate versions of the Ami 6. In 1966, they gained 12-volt electrics and an alternator. Cars built from 1967 onwards can be recognised by their new design of front grille, with three horizontal bars. For the 1968 model year, the engine was uprated to 27.5bhp and a new, top-of-the-range Club trim added for the estate (the Club saloon followed suit for the 1969 model year). All Club models were fitted with four round headlamps, new 'Gala' wheel trims and side rubbing strips similar to those on the DS Pallas. The interior of the Club models was more luxurious, with carpets instead of rubber mats, reclining front seats and mixed cloth and leatherette upholstery. Also for the 1968 model year, all Ami 6 saloons received a new trapezoidal rear light design, which was subsequently adopted on

(All courtesy Citroën Communication)

Citroën Cars 1934 to 1986 – A Pictorial History

The Ami 6 estate had far more conventional rear styling than the saloon. (All three photographs courtesy Citroën Communication)

the 2CV in 1970, and a fabric sunroof became available as an option.

In May 1968, a new M28 engine was fitted: it kept the same layout and 602cc capacity, but power increased to 35bhp (SAE). At the same time, Citroën presented a tax-saving three-door van model for business users: the Service. Initially, this had metal side panels, but from June 1968 a version with rear side windows was also offered. In March 1969, the

Ami and M35

saloon made way for the new Ami 8, followed by the estate in September that year.

NUMBER PRODUCED: 483,986 (saloon); 551,880 (estate); 3519 (Service).
PRICE AT LAUNCH: 6550FF.
ENGINE: Air-cooled, two-cylinder (flat-twin) petrol, OHV layout. Bore 74mm, stroke 70mm, capacity 602cc, maximum power 22bhp (SAE) at 4500rpm (1961-1964); 25.5bhp (SAE) at 4750rpm (1965-1967); 27.5bhp (SAE) at 5400rpm (1967-1968); 35bhp (SAE) at 5750rpm (1968-1969). Solex carburettor.
TRANSMISSION: Front-wheel drive, four-speed manual gearbox, dashboard-mounted gearlever. Final drive ratio: 3.625:1; gear ratios: first 6.00:1; second 3.13:1; third 1.92:1; fourth 1.42:1. Optional centrifugal clutch.
BRAKES: Front: inboard drums; rear: drums.
TYRES: 125 X 380 (135 X 380 on five-seat estate and Commerciale).
SUSPENSION: Fully independent but interconnected front to rear with longitudinal coil springs, inertia and friction dampers.
STEERING: Rack and pinion.

DIMENSIONS: Length: 3.87-3.96m/152.4-155.9in (estate: 3.89m/153.0in); width: 1.52m (59.8in); height: 1.49m (58.7in); wheelbase: 2.40m (94.5in); turning circle (between kerbs): 11m (36.1ft).
KERB WEIGHT: 620-640kg/1367-1411lb (estate: 704kg/1552lb).
CAPACITIES: Fuel: 25l (5.5gal); boot: $0.33m^3/11.7ft^3$ (estate: $1.50m^3/53ft^3$ with seats folded).
COLOURS:
1961 Gris Liban, Bleu Avril, Blanc Carrare, Vert Absinthe.
1969 Gris Rosé, Bleu Danube, Blanc Albâtre, Bleu Mésange, Rouge Cornaline, Jaune Bouton d'Or, Or Sombre, Vert Iris.

Club model with four round headlamps. (Right: courtesy Citroën Communication)

Ami 8

Following Flaminio Bertoni's death in 1964, it fell to Robert Opron to design the Ami 6's successor: the Ami 8. The front end was simplified on both the saloon and estate. While the design of the estate was otherwise similar to that of the Ami 6, the saloon was more extensively restyled, with a more consensual fastback design. It still had a conventional separate boot opening, however, rather than a hatchback. Inside, there was a completely new dashboard and the front doors each had an armrest and map pocket.

Two trim levels were offered when the saloon was launched at the Geneva Motor Show in March 1969: the basic Confort model, and, as with the Ami 6, a better equipped Club version. The Club had stainless steel window trim, side rubbing strips, cloth and leatherette upholstery and separate front seats with reclining backrests, as well as interior carpets and a fully lined boot. Unlike the Ami 6 Club, however, it no longer had four headlamps or 'Gala' wheel trims. Front and rear seatbelts, a radio and (on Confort models) separate front seats were listed as options. Mechanically, the new car was very similar to the outgoing model with the M28 engine, but the gear ratios were slightly changed and a larger fuel tank and front anti-roll bar were fitted. A centrifugal clutch was optional.

The Ami 8 estate made its début in September 1969 and offered a useful payload of 735kg (1620lb), as well as a completely flat load floor. Unsurprisingly, it was again a success, outselling the Ami 8 saloon over its lifetime. Confort and Club versions were available from the start, as was a three-door Service van. At the same time as the estate was presented, front disc brakes and a new master cylinder were fitted across the range, and the braking system used the LHM fluid introduced on the DS in 1966. Some slight

Publicity photo from the launch of the Ami 8. (Courtesy Citroën Communication)

Ami and M35

Unlike its saloon counterpart, the rear styling of the Ami 8 estate was little changed from that of the Ami 6.

modifications were made to the cars' trim and mechanical specification.

In 1970, the biggest change was the introduction of wind-down front windows, unfortunately leaving no space for front door pockets. Cars built after June 1970 had a double chevron motif on the front grille. Over the next few years, there was a steady flow of mechanical and electrical changes, many of them relatively minor, as Citroën upgraded specific components or changed suppliers. One significant modification, however, was made in 1972, when the rear inertia dampers were replaced by hydraulic shock absorbers. The cars' appearance evolved relatively little, but in 1971 halogen headlamps became an option, and at the start of 1973 there was a new design of padded steering wheel. In September 1973, the colour of the dashboard changed from black to Havana (brown), but its basic layout remained the same. For 1974, the saloon gained the wider 135-section tyres already fitted to the estates.

By 1976, the end of the Ami's career was in sight. That year, the version of the Service van with rear side windows was dropped, as was the Ami Super (see below). For 1977, Citroën nonetheless made some final improvements to the cars' equipment, with dual-circuit brakes, separate front seats and a folding back seat standard across the range. In July 1977, inertia-reel front seatbelts also became standard. The panelled Service van was renamed the Entreprise. Production of the Ami 8 – which had been built in Spain and Argentina as well as France – came to an end at the beginning of 1979, when it was succeeded by the Visa.

NUMBER PRODUCED: 342,743 (saloon); 386,582 (estate); 26,630 (Service/Entreprise).

ENGINE: Air-cooled, two-cylinder (flat-twin) petrol, OHV layout. Bore 74mm, stroke 70mm, capacity 602cc, maximum power 32bhp (DIN) at 5750rpm, Solex 26/35 SCIC twin-choke carburettor (34 PICS 6 from 1972).

TRANSMISSION: Front-wheel drive, four-

1974 Ami 8 interior. (Courtesy Peter Singhof – Artcurial Motorcars)

speed manual gearbox, dashboard-mounted gearlever. Final drive ratio: 3.875:1; gear ratios: first 5.75:1; second 2.94:1; third 1.92:1; fourth 1.35:1. Optional centrifugal clutch.
BRAKES: Front: inboard discs (from 09/1969); rear: drums.
TYRES: 125 X 380; 135 X 380 on estates, and on saloons from 09/1973.
SUSPENSION: Fully independent but interconnected front to rear with longitudinal coil springs; front: anti-roll bar; rear: inertia dampers until 1972, then hydraulic shock absorbers.
STEERING: Rack and pinion.
DIMENSIONS: Length: 3.99m (157.1in); width: 1.55m (61.2in); height: 1.49m (58.8in); wheelbase: 2.40m (94.5in); turning circle (between kerbs): 11.4m (37.4ft).
KERB WEIGHT: 725kg (1598lb).
CAPACITIES: Fuel: 32l (7.0gal); boot: 0.29m³/10.2ft³ (estate: 0.45m³/15.8ft³ and 1.20m³/42.3ft³ with rear seats folded; van: 1.42m³/50.3ft³).

Ami Super

In January 1973, Citroën extended the Ami range when it introduced the Ami Super, available in saloon, estate, Commerciale and Service body styles. Confort and Club trim levels were available. For the first time, the A-Series platform was home to a four-cylinder engine – the all-alloy overhead cam unit from the GS 1015 – developing 54bhp (DIN). This was mated to the four-speed manual gearbox from the GS 1220 with a floor-mounted gear change, and there was a larger fuel tank. The braking system (with standard front discs from the GS) was uprated and the chassis strengthened. Bigger shock absorbers and front and rear anti-roll bars were fitted, but the suspension was no longer interconnected from front to rear. The Super was praised by the press at the time for its surprising turn of speed and good roadholding, making it something of a 'Q-car.'

Externally, the Ami Super could be distinguished from the Ami 8 by its new front

Two views of the Ami Super estate.

Ami and M35

grille with a decorative strip and six additional cooling slats underneath. Stainless steel window trim and side rubbing strips were fitted, as on the Ami 8 Club. There was a small '1015' badge on the right front wing, later replaced by an 'Ami Super' badge. The wheels initially came from the Ami 8, but had a distinctive slotted design from 1974; at the same time, a black stripe along the side of the car (unique to the Super) was added. Inside, the Club had mixed jersey (cloth) and leatherette trim, separate reclining front seats and carpets with a heel pad for the driver. A range of options was available: a Blaupunkt radio, heated rear window, rear seatbelts, halogen headlamps and metallic paint.

There were few changes to the Ami Super's specification during its career, but in 1975 uprated 135 SR 15 ZX tyres were fitted and hazard warning lights added. Compared with the Ami 6 and Ami 8, it was not a great success, with fewer than 45,000 cars built in all. It undoubtedly suffered in its home market from its steep fiscal horsepower rating (6CV) and relatively high fuel consumption. The Service van – a massive flop – was the first version to be discontinued, soon followed by the saloon and estate in 1976.

NUMBER PRODUCED: 24,797 (saloon); 19,222 (estate); 801 (Service).

ENGINE: Air-cooled, four-cylinder (flat-four) petrol, SOHC design. Bore 74mm, stroke 59mm, capacity 1015cc, maximum power 54bhp (DIN) at 6500rpm, Solex 28 CIC twin-choke carburettor.
TRANSMISSION: Front-wheel drive, four-speed manual gearbox with synchromesh on all gears, floor-mounted gearlever. Final drive ratio: 4.125:1; gear ratios: first 3.81:1; second 2.31:1; third 1.52:1; fourth 1.12:1.
BRAKES: Front: inboard discs; rear: drums.
TYRES: 135 X 15.
SUSPENSION: Fully independent, with hydraulic shock absorbers; front and rear anti-roll bars.
STEERING: Rack and pinion.
DIMENSIONS: as Ami 8.
KERB WEIGHT: 815kg (1797lb).
CAPACITIES: Fuel: 40l (8.8gal); boot: as Ami 8.

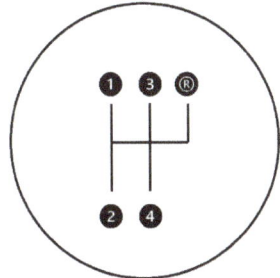

Gear change layout for the Ami Super.

M35

During the early 1960s, Citroën was one of several carmakers interested in the potential of rotary engines. In 1964, it established a new company, Comobile, with the German firm NSU, which held the rights to the Wankel engine. Its ultimate goal was to develop a jointly produced car, combining the innovative approach to design of both its parent companies. The first product of this project was the Citroën M35, presented in November 1969 as a mobile test bed for the new technology. The engine for the M35 was built by NSU and designated the KKM 613; it was based on the older single-rotor engine used in the NSU Spider. It was far more powerful than the flat-twin fitted to the Ami 8, and had a rev counter and buzzer to guard against over-revving. The engine was mated to the four-speed manual transmission from the GS 1015 with the Ami's traditional dashboard-mounted gearlever, but higher gear ratios enabled the car to reach nearly 130km/h (80mph) in third. Nor did the M35's technical innovations stop there, as it also featured Citroën's hydropneumatic suspension, as used on the DS.

The body was based on the Ami 8, although the only components it shared with it were the front wings. The French coachbuilder Heuliez designed a unique 2+2 fastback coupé for the M35, with longer front doors and a large sloping rear screen. Most of the cars were finished in metallic grey, a few in metallic blue; all had black vinyl interiors with a new design of reclining seats that would also be adopted in the SM.

The M35 was not sold as part of Citroën's normal range; instead, it was supplied to some of the company's favoured customers across France to carry out a long-term test. Preference was given to high-mileage drivers covering 30,000km (18,600 miles) or more per year. At the end of the test, Citroën took back most of the cars and they were scrapped. It was planned to build 500 cars, but in the end only 267 were completed from 1969-1971, each of them individually numbered. The cars suffered many problems with premature rotor wear, starting and overall reliability, but the company continued its development programme, which led to the launch of the GS Birotor in 1973.

NUMBER PRODUCED: 267.
PRICE AT LAUNCH: 14,000FF.
ENGINE: Water-cooled, single-rotor Wankel-type petrol. Capacity 497.5cc (rated as equivalent to 995cc piston engine), maximum power 49bhp (DIN) at 5500rpm, Solex 18/32 HHD carburettor.
TRANSMISSION: Front-wheel drive, four-

Ami and M35

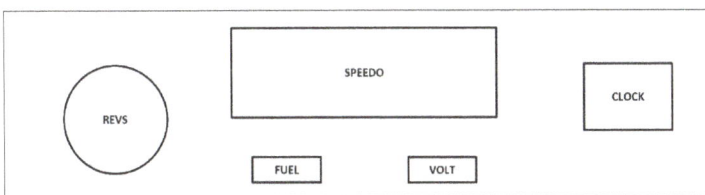

Dashboard and gear change layout for the M35.

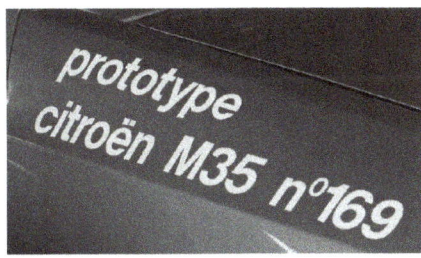

speed manual gearbox, dashboard-mounted gearlever. Final drive ratio: 4.125:1; gear ratios first 3.82:1; second 2.31:1; third 1.45:1; fourth 1.08:1.
BRAKES: Front: inboard discs; rear: drums.
TYRES: 135 X15.
SUSPENSION: Fully independent self-levelling hydropneumatic, with anti-roll bars at front and rear.

STEERING: Rack and pinion.
DIMENSIONS: Length: 4.05m (159.4in); width: 1.54m (61.2in); height: 1.35m (53.1in); wheelbase: 2.40m (94.5in); turning circle (between kerbs): 11.4m (37.4ft).
KERB WEIGHT: 815kg (1797lb).
CAPACITIES: Fuel: 43l (9.5gal); boot: 0.31m^3 (10.9ft^3).
COLOURS: Gris Nacré, Bleu Delta.

GS and GSA

Although the Ami 6 proved a commercial success, it was far closer to the basic 2CV than the ID, and left Citroën with a continuing gap in its range during the 1960s. After a couple of false starts to create a new midrange model, in 1967 it urgently began work on 'Projet G,' with flat-four (GX) and rotary-engined (GZ) versions planned.

Presented at the 1970 Paris Motor Show, the new front-wheel drive GS carried over the flat-four, air-cooled engine originally planned for 'Projet F' – which had been hastily abandoned in 1967 – but with an increased capacity of 1015cc. The GS was technically advanced, with hydraulic systems for its all-round disc brakes and self-levelling suspension. The model's four-door saloon body was designed by Robert Opron, who made extensive use of aerodynamic principles to compensate for the car's relatively small engine. With the help of its fastback lines and Kamm tail, the GS had the best drag coefficient (0.32) of any car on sale at the time of its launch. Pierre Bercot, Citroën's managing director, remained hostile to hatchback designs, so it had a conventional boot with a low opening (the bumper was actually part of the lid). The GS was well received and was elected European

(Courtesy Citroën Communication)

Car of the Year 1971. The company celebrated its success with the 'Voiture sans Frontières' limited edition that year, but only a few dozen were built.

During the 1970s, the GS range progressively expanded, with larger engines, different trim levels and estate and van versions. In 1972, Bertone proposed a 2+2 coupé based on the GS: the Camargue, designed by Marcello Gandini. It was exhibited at the Geneva Motor Show but never made it into production. The 1015cc flat-four engine also found its way into the short-lived BFG motorbike and the single-seater MEP

(Courtesy Citroën Communication)

GS and GSA

(Courtesy Citroën Communication)

X27 racing cars created by Maurice Emile Pezous, a Citroën dealer from Albi. 25 MEP X27s were built for the first 'Formule Bleu' single-make series in 1971, followed by a second run the next year. In 1973, Citroën launched the remarkable GS Birotor, with a twin-rotor Wankel engine, following on from the experimental M35.

In 1979, the GS was replaced by the GSA and the saloon finally received a hatchback. The GSA continued on sale in France until 1986, when it was supplanted by the lower-

The GS Camargue concept car.

MEP X27s at the Circuit des Remparts in Angoulême.

GS saloons coming down the production line at Rennes-la-Janais. (Courtesy Citroën Communication)

spec BX models. In all, nearly 2.5 million GS and GSAs were built, most of them at Rennes-la-Janais in Brittany. It was also produced at Vigo in Spain, where 385,000 cars were built, and in smaller numbers in Portugal, Yugoslavia, South Africa, Rhodesia (later Zimbabwe), Chile and Indonesia.

GS

At its launch in September 1970, the GS saloon was available in two trim levels: Confort and Club. The Club was better equipped, with cloth seats (reclining in the front), carpets, extra brightwork and bumper overriders; metallic paint and front headrests were optional. The GS was praised for its excellent ride and handling, as well as for its spacious boot and interior, but the 55.5bhp (DIN) 1-litre engine was considered too low-powered and thirsty. Cars sold in the UK had a conventional dashboard with round Jaeger instruments rather than the more futuristic layout used in other markets.

In February 1971, a three-speed semi-automatic gearbox (initially known as 'Convertisseur,' and from 1975 as 'C-matic') was offered as an alternative to the four-speed manual; the clutch was actuated by touching the gearknob rather than by a conventional third pedal. In September that year, the five-door estate joined the range, with Confort and Club versions again available. Alongside the estate, Citroën introduced a tax-saving Commerciale model for business users (with the rear doors welded shut and no rear seats) and a three-door Service van, which could carry up to 445kg (981lb). The Confort version of this had metal side panels, but the stylish Club version sported full-length rear side windows and a laminated load floor. In the

Leatherette trim and optional headrests. (Courtesy Citroën Communication)

UK, small numbers of the Service model were sold as the GS 8.5cwt van, in Confort, Super Confort and Club trim levels. Ambulance and police versions were also sold in France.

In September 1972, Citroën responded to criticism that the GS was underpowered and introduced a larger 1222cc engine (models with this engine are generally referred to as the 1220). This developed only slightly more power (60bhp), but at lower revs, resulting in less wear and better economy. At this point, the 1015 became available only in Confort trim and with the manual gearbox, the Club trim and 'Convertisseur' transmission now being reserved for the 1220. The larger-engined cars could be recognised by their '1220' badges on the right front wing, boot and dashboard. Tinted glass and new models of Blaupunkt radio (mounted vertically between the seats, as

Unconventional dashboard layout for cars sold in Continental Europe. (Courtesy Citroën Communication)

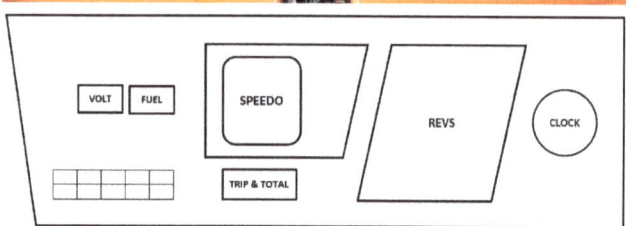

As on the saloon, the rear bumper of the estate lifted as part of the tailgate (Courtesy Citroën Communication/Jean Peyrin)

on the SM) could be ordered as options, and there were minor changes to trim and interior equipment on all models.

In September 1973, the slow-selling Commerciale model was discontinued, but the big news for the 1974 model year was the introduction of the GS Birotor. In January 1974, the Confort models were renamed G Spécial. A few months later, in September 1974, Citroën widened the GS range, adding three new saloon-only models. The GS X (1015cc) and X2 (1222cc) were intended to appeal to younger buyers and had a sportier look, with a black front grille, additional long-range driving lamps, and small hubcaps (initially black). Inside, both models had black 'Targa' upholstery and rally-style seats with integrated headrests, as well as a new dashboard with round Jaeger dials including a rev counter. The engine of the GS X was unchanged, but for the X2 it was uprated from 60bhp to 64bhp (DIN). Optional shorter ratios for the manual gearbox provided quicker acceleration. In South Africa, an additional X2 Le Mans model was offered, with an uprated

GS and GSA

GS X2 dashboard. (Courtesy Citromuseum/ Henri Fradet)

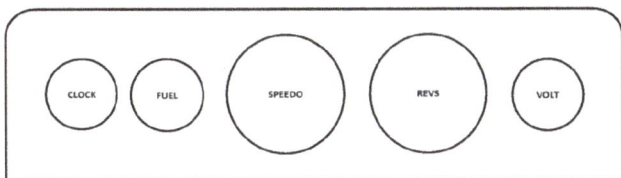

engine, twin stripes along the sides, four round headlamps, a rear spoiler and rear window louvres.

The Pallas (available only with the 1222cc engine) was the new top-of-the-range model, inspired by the successful DS Pallas: it had a more luxurious interior with different cloth upholstery, a brown rather than black dashboard, metal sill plates and map pockets on the front seat backrests. A heated rear window was fitted as standard. Externally, the Pallas could be identified by its large disc-type wheel trims and side rubbing strips; a vinyl roof was optional.

There were few changes for the rest of 1975 and the 1976 model year, with the

exception of the fitment of new carburettors in 1976 to lessen exhaust emissions: these had the effect of reducing power by 0.5bhp (1015cc)/1bhp (1222cc). In September 1976, however, Citroën facelifted the entire GS range. The revised models had four-section taillights, a new instrument panel with three round dials and a centre console. The Club and Pallas models were now equipped with halogen headlamps and had a new grille with three horizontal bars. The Club estate was fitted with a rear wash/wipe as standard, while the Service van was renamed the Entreprise. The facelifted X and X2 models could be identified by their black bumpers, and from 1975-1978 Citroën reserved one special colour each year for these two models. The X2 even inspired a French artist, Jean-Pierre Lihou, to create an 'Art Car,' officially known as the GS Energétique, but often referred to as the GS 'Aux flèches' on account of the arrows in 73 different colours painted on its bodywork.

In September 1977, for the 1978 model year, there were changes to the design of wheel trims and front grille (which now had vertical slats). The X and X2 models received a number of upgrades: the long-range driving lamps were replaced by foglamps fitted below the front bumper and the rear seat gained a folding centre armrest; in addition, the X2 now had a rear spoiler and halogen headlamps. On the G Spécial and GS Club saloons, a fold-down rear seat was listed as an option, a first step towards the greater modularity the GSA would provide. The biggest change was

Post-facelift dashboard. (Courtesy Citroën Communication)

the replacement of the original 1015cc engine by a new 1129cc unit, based on the longer-stroke 1222cc engine: this was still rated at 6CV in France, but now developed 56bhp (DIN). Models with this engine are sometimes referred to as the 1130.

In April 1978, following a proposal made by Heuliez, Citroën presented the limited-edition GS Basalte. 1800 were produced for France and 1500 for Germany, where it was called the Basalt. Based on the 1220 Club, it had distinctive black paintwork with red stripes, and matching black-and-red houndstooth cloth upholstery with black carpets. It was very well equipped, with tinted glass, a laminated windscreen, sunroof, foglamps, Pallas-type wheel trims, headrests and a radio/cassette player as standard. It proved a huge success, selling out in France in just two weeks.

Promotional photo for the facelifted GS Pallas. (Courtesy Citroën Communication)

GS X2 in Rouge Soleil, available only in 1977. (Courtesy Citroën Communication)

Below: Jean-Pierre Lihou's GS 'Aux flèches.'

The 1979 model year would be the last full year for the GS. Inertia-reel front seatbelts and two static rear belts were fitted, and there were changes to the upholstery on the GS X and Club. The X2, however, was dropped, to be replaced by a new X3 model in September 1978. This was very similar to the outgoing X2 (with the addition of side rubbing strips), but inaugurated the larger 1299cc engine which would power the GSA range (see GSA section below for technical data). 34,862 1299cc-engined GS saloons were built, and a further 800 1299cc GS estates were sold in Switzerland. After the GSA was announced in July 1979, the G Spécial and GS Entreprise persevered with the old body style for another few months, until they too were replaced by the equivalent GSA models in July 1980.

GS 1015

NUMBER PRODUCED: 447,631 (saloon); 76,745 (estate); 6235 (Service/Entreprise).
PRICES AT LAUNCH: 11,380FF (Confort); 12,200FF (Club).
ENGINE: Air-cooled, four-cylinder (flat-four) petrol, SOHC design. Bore 74mm, stroke 59mm, capacity 1015cc, maximum power 55.5bhp (DIN) at 6500rpm (55bhp at 6500rpm from 1976), Solex 28 CIC twin-choke carburettor.
TRANSMISSION: Front-wheel drive, four-speed manual gearbox with synchromesh on all gears, floor-mounted gearlever. Final drive ratio: 4.375:1; gear ratios: first 3.82:1; second 2.38:1; third 1.52:1; fourth 1.12:1. Three-speed semi-automatic transmission

GS Basalte. (Courtesy Citromuseum/ Henri Fradet)

GS X3 from 1979. (Courtesy Citroën Communication)

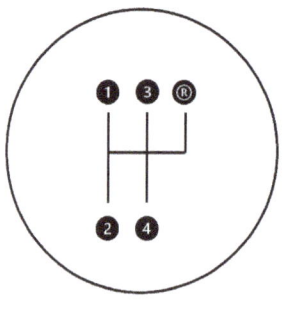

Four-speed manual gear layout.

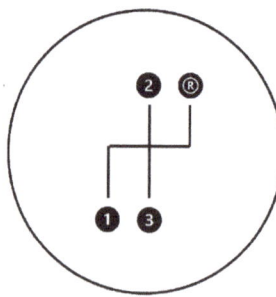

Three-speed C-matic gear layout.

GS and GSA

with Verto torque converter optional (1971-1972).
BRAKES: Front: inboard discs; rear: discs. Hydraulic servo control and dual circuits.
TYRES: 145 SR 15.
SUSPENSION: Fully independent, self-levelling hydropneumatic with anti-squat geometry and front and rear anti-roll bars. Front: double wishbones; rear: trailing arms.
STEERING: Rack and pinion.
DIMENSIONS (saloon and estate): Length: 4.12m (162.2in); width: 1.61m (63.4in); height: 1.35m (53.1in); wheelbase: 2.55m (100.4in); turning circle (between kerbs): 9.4m (30.8ft).
KERB WEIGHT: 880kg/1940lb (estate: 935kg/2061lb; Service/Entreprise: 895kg/1973lb).
CAPACITIES: Fuel: 43l (9.5gal); boot: 0.465m³/16.4ft³ (estate: 0.71m³/25.1ft³ and 1.51m³/53.3ft³ with rear seats folded; Service/Entreprise: 1.66m³/58.6ft³).

GS 1220

KEY DIFFERENCES
NUMBER PRODUCED: 864,759 (saloon); 268,240 (estate); 7985 (Service/Entreprise).
PRICES AT LAUNCH: 13,700FF (saloon); 14,300FF (estate); 14,932FF (Service van with side windows).
ENGINE: Bore 77mm, stroke 65.6mm, capacity 1222cc, maximum power 60bhp (DIN) at 5750rpm (59bhp at 6500rpm from 1976); X2: 65bhp (DIN) at 6500rpm (64bhp from 1976), Solex 28 CIC twin-choke carburettor.
TRANSMISSION: Final drive ratio: 4.125:1; gear ratios as GS 1015. Three-speed semi-automatic transmission optional: Final drive ratio: 4.125:1; gear ratios: first 2.79:1; second 1.70:1; third 1.12:1.
KERB WEIGHT: 900kg/1984lb (estate: 940kg/2072lb; Service/Entreprise: 900kg/1984lb).

GS 1130

KEY DIFFERENCES
NUMBER PRODUCED: 136,259 (saloon); 45,158 (estate); 7768 (Entreprise).
PRICES AT LAUNCH: 23,160FF (G Spécial saloon); 24,760FF (G Spécial estate); 20,450 (Entreprise).
ENGINE: Bore 74mm, stroke 65.6mm, capacity 1129cc, maximum power 56bhp (DIN) at 5750rpm, Weber twin-choke carburettor.
TRANSMISSION: Final drive ratio: 4.125:1; gear ratios: first 3.82:1; second 2.29:1; third 1.50:1; fourth 1.03:1.
KERB WEIGHT: 925kg/2039lb (estate: 935kg/2061lb).

COLOURS (All GS models):
Beige Nevada, Beige Opale, Beige Gazelle, Beige Vanneau, Ivoire Borély, Gris d'Anjou, Beige Albatros, Blanc Meije, Beige Erable, Gris Nacré (Pallas only until 1979), Noir, Bronze,, Jaune Primevère, Jaune Hélianthe (X/X2 only), Orange Ténéré (G Spécial only), Jaune Cédrat, Orange Ibiza (X/X2 only), Jaune Mimosa, Rouge Masséna, Rouge de Rio, Brun Scarabée, Rouge Soleil (X/X2 only), Brun de Santal, Brun des Andes, Rouge Géranium, Brun Cigale, Brun Vésuve, Vert Charmille, Vert Argenté, Vert Nopal, Vert Papyrus, Vert Reinette, Bleu Thasos, Bleu Platiné, Bleu Camargue, Bleu Grignan, Bleu Lagune, Bleu Delta, Bleu Hunaudières (X/X2 only), Bleu Pétrel, Bleu Régate, Bleu Myosotis, Bleu Gentiane.

GS Birotor

Presented at the Frankfurt Motor Show in September 1973, the GS Birotor was a big step forwards from the experimental M35. The smooth power delivery of the free-revving twin-rotor engine, mated to a semi-automatic transmission (the same combination as in the NSU Ro80), was a good match for the smooth-riding GS. The Comotor rotary engine produced 107bhp (DIN), giving the new model comparable performance to the DS 23, but in a more compact and modern package. Power-assisted steering was the only notable omission from its advanced specification.

Externally, the Birotor could be recognised by its flared wheelarches, grey radiator grille with gold chevrons, stainless steel exhaust tailpipe, special rotary badges on the front wing and boot lid, and grey-painted wheels with distinctive concave hubcaps and wider tyres. Initially, it was available in brown and/or beige, either in a single colour or with a brown roof and beige body, or vice versa. Inside, the Birotor featured Jaeger instruments and hazelnut-coloured jersey upholstery; the front seats had integrated headrests similar to those of the GS X and X2. An oil level gauge at the base of the centre console was a key addition, as the Wankel had higher oil consumption than piston engines. Tinted glass, a sunroof and various models of radio were listed as options, as well as rear seatbelts (curiously, only until July 1974).

The Birotor officially went on sale in France in March 1974 but was never sold in the UK or in right-hand drive. A few changes were made from August for the 1975 model year: a new shade of brown and three additional colours became available, and a vinyl roof was added to the options list. Inside, all the cars had hazelnut-coloured upholstery, regardless of the exterior colour, and the cloth trim was extended to the door cards.

Despite its many qualities, the Birotor

was penalised by its high price – which brought it into competition with cars from the class above such as the Peugeot 504 Ti automatic or Citroën's own DS 23 – its fiscal horsepower rating (11CV) and, not least, its fuel consumption (higher even than the DS 23 IE). The timing of its launch at the start of

Brochure shot of the GS Birotor. (Courtesy Citroën Communication)

GS and GSA

the oil crisis could scarcely have been worse. Reliability issues due to premature seal wear on the rotary engine also soon became apparent.

Altogether, Citroën built 847 cars before production came to an end early in 1975, but many remained unsold and were given to the company's top dealers for their personal use, on the condition that they would not be resold. Eventually – no doubt fearful of the cost of guaranteeing the supply of spare parts for ten years, as was legally required – Citroën recalled the cars, offering the few private buyers generous part-exchange deals on the CX. The chassis plates and engines were removed, and, in the end (as late as 1986), the cars were scrapped. As many as 50 examples of the Birotor have nonetheless survived. Citroën carried out some development work for a potential three-rotor CX, but this was shelved by Peugeot, and the company would never build another rotary-engined car.

NUMBER PRODUCED: 847.
PRICE AT LAUNCH: 24,952FF.
ENGINE: Water-cooled, twin-rotor Wankel-type petrol (Comotor type 624). Capacity 995cc (rated as equivalent to 1990cc piston engine), maximum power 107bhp (DIN) at 6500rpm, Solex 32 DDITS twin-choke carburettor.
TRANSMISSION: Three-speed semi-automatic with hydraulic torque converter, floor-mounted selector. Final drive ratio: 4.25:1; gear ratios: first 2.1:1; second 1.30:1; third 0.91:1.
BRAKES: Front: ventilated discs; rear: solid discs. Hydraulic servo control and dual circuits.
TYRES: 165 HR 14.
SUSPENSION: Fully independent, self-levelling hydropneumatic with front and rear anti-roll bars. Front: double wishbones, anti-squat geometry; rear: trailing arms.
STEERING: Rack and pinion.
DIMENSIONS: Length: 4.12m (162.2in); width: 1.64m (64.6in); height: 1.37m (53.9in); wheelbase: 2.55m (100.5in); turning circle (between kerbs): 10.6m (34.8ft).
KERB WEIGHT: 1140kg (2513lb).
CAPACITIES: Fuel: 56l (12.3gal); boot: 0.465m^3/16.4ft^3.
COLOURS:
1973-1974 Beige Tholonet, Brun Scarabée.
1974-1975 Brun de Santal, Brun Scarabée, Bleu Delta, Gris Nacré, Vert Nopal.

GS Birotor badge.
(Courtesy Citroën Communication)

119

Citroën Cars 1934 to 1986 – A Pictorial History

GSA

When the GSA went on sale in September 1979, Citroën's midrange saloon finally gained the hatchback it needed to be competitive. The car's overall styling was similar to the GS, but the plastic bumpers, front grille, side rubbing strips, wheel trims and door handles were all new. Inside, the GSA had a brand-new dashboard which proved that the company's individualistic approach to design had not been lost. Like the CX, the GSA sported a pair of control pods on either side of the steering wheel, grouping together the different controls for lights, wipers and indicators. Citroën referred to these as PRN satellites, for 'Pluie' (Rain), 'Route' (Road) and 'Nuit' (Night). The instrument panel was just as unconventional, with rotating drums (again like the CX) for road speed and engine revs, below an array of warning lights linked to a large schematic diagram of the car. In the UK, however, the old-style dash from the GS continued for another year. The radio, when fitted, was still mounted vertically between the seats.

The GSA launched as a saloon in Club, Pallas and X3 trim, and as a Club estate, all with the 1299cc engine developing 65bhp (DIN) introduced the previous year in the GS X3. In Spain, an ambulance model with a raised roof was also offered. The GSA X3 had a five-speed manual gearbox with a shorter final drive ratio as standard; the Club and Pallas had a four-speed manual gearbox, with a five-speeder (with standard ratios) optional. The C-matic semi-automatic transmission also continued as an option until July 1983. Options included a rear wash/wipe, sunroof, alloy wheels and tinted glass (green until 1981, then bronze); front headrests were available as dealer-fit accessories.

In July 1980, the G Spécial and GS Entreprise were replaced by the GSA Spécial and the GSA Entreprise panelled van. The GSA Spécial had slightly more basic trim than the Club and was initially fitted with the 1129cc engine. There were minor changes to the existing GSA models and a rear wash/wipe and interior adjustment for the passenger door mirror became standard on the X3.

In July 1981, for the 1982 model year, the range was reconfigured. The GSA Spécial received the 1299cc engine, and a clock and carpets became standard. Beneath it, Citroën introduced a base-spec GSA with the 1129cc engine and the simplest trim, but this was discontinued after only two years. The Entreprise van was also fitted with the 1299cc engine. Now designated '1300 ECO,'

The GSA range. (Courtesy Citroën Communication)

GS and GSA

Interior of a GSA Spécial. (Courtesy Citroën Communication) Dashboard layout below.

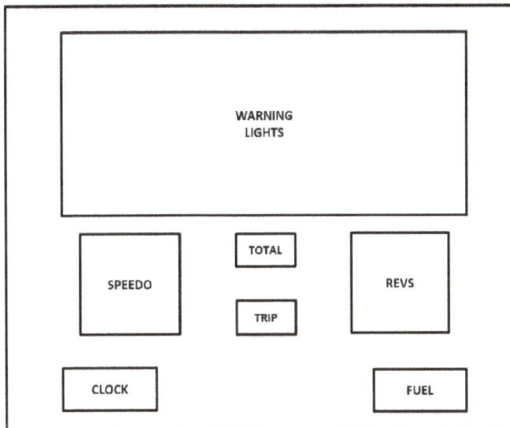

the 1299cc engine was revised throughout the range to lower fuel consumption, but power fell by 1bhp to 64bhp (DIN). In April 1982, Citroën introduced the GSA Tuner, its first limited edition. 1500 examples of this were produced, finished in black with blue and silver stripes. Mechanically, it was based on the Club saloon with a five-speed manual gearbox. Standard equipment included tinted glass, front headrests and a sophisticated Philips audio system.

There was a further change to the range for the 1983 model year, when the Club saloon was replaced by the X1. This was very similar in appearance to the X3, but some items of standard equipment (such as the rear central armrest and the map pockets in the front seat backrests) were dropped, while others (such as the five-speed gearbox or rear wash/wipe) became optional. The 1983 model year also saw improvements to the Pallas saloon, which gained front headrests, and to

GSA Club saloon and estate. (Estate photo courtesy Citroën Communication)

GSA Pallas saloon. (Courtesy Citroën Communication)

GSA Entreprise van. (Courtesy Citroën Communication)

the Club estate, which now had a carpeted load compartment.

At the end of 1983, production of the GSA transferred from Brittany to Vigo in Spain. After this, production continued until 1986, with a final batch of Entreprise vans built in Indonesia in 1987. There were hardly any further changes of note other than the adoption of the shorter gear ratios from the X3 for all five-speed manuals in July 1984. Citroën did, however, try to boost sales of the model with two more limited editions. The first of these, presented in September 1983, was the GSA Cottage, based on the Club estate with a five-speed manual gearbox. 1850 cars were built, all finished in a shade of metallic gold delightfully known as Beige Sloughi, set off by orange and brown stripes. It had 'Melrose' tweed upholstery, a removable load cover and the alloy wheels from the X3. The Cottage was followed in July 1984 by the GSA Chic, of which 1200 were built. Based this time on the GSA Spécial with a five-speed manual transmission, it had metallic grey paint (Gris Perlé) with red pinstripes and tartan

GSA X1. (Courtesy Citroën Communication)

GS and GSA

*GSA Cottage.
(Courtesy Citromuseum/Henri Fradet)*

upholstery; alloy wheels, a rear spoiler, tinted glass and front headrests were all standard. For its final year, Citroën simplified the range, leaving only the GSA Spécial and X3 saloon, GSA Spécial estate and GSA Entreprise van on sale from July 1985.
NUMBER PRODUCED: 477,960 (saloon); 87,063 (estate); 11,748 (Entreprise).
PRICES AT LAUNCH: 33,600FF-35,900FF (saloons); 34,800FF (Club estate).
ENGINE: Air-cooled, four-cylinder (flat-four) petrol, single OHC per bank. Bore 79.4mm, stroke 65.6mm, capacity 1299cc, maximum power 65bhp (DIN) at 5500rpm (64bhp from 07/81), Solex or Weber twin-choke carburettor.
TRANSMISSION: Front-wheel drive, four- or five-speed manual gearbox with synchromesh on all gears, floor-mounted gearlever. Final drive ratio: 4.125:1 (short-ratio five-speed: 4.375:1); gear ratios (five-speed): first 3.82:1; second 2.29:1; third 1.50:1; fourth 1.13:1; fifth 0.91:1. Three-speed semi-automatic transmission optional (until 07/1983).
BRAKES: Front: ventilated inboard discs; rear: solid discs. Hydraulic servo control and dual circuits.
TYRES: 145 SR 15.
SUSPENSION: Fully independent, self-levelling hydropneumatic with front and rear anti-roll bars. Front: double wishbones, anti-squat geometry; rear: trailing arms.
STEERING: Rack and pinion.
DIMENSIONS: Length: 4.19m/165.2in (estate: 4.16m/163.6in); width: 1.63m (64.0in); height: 1.35m (53.1in); wheelbase: 2.55m (100.4in); turning circle (between kerbs): 9.7m (31.7ft).

KERB WEIGHT: 955kg/2105lb (estate: 965kg/2127lb).
CAPACITIES: Fuel: 43l (9.5gal); boot: 0.435m^3/15.4ft^3 (estate: 0.645m^3/22.8ft^3 and 1.504m^3/53.1ft^3 with rear seats folded; Entreprise: 1.66m^3/58.6ft^3).
COLOURS: Beige Daim, Gris Requin, Beige Colorado, Gris Perlé, Blanc Meije, Gris Nacré, Noir, Rouge Géranium, Brun Vésuve, Cuivre Tammela, Cuivre Pargas, Vert Jade, Vert Tamaris, Vert Chevreuse, Bleu Platiné, Bleu Camargue, Bleu Lagune, Bleu Régate, Bleu Azurite, Bleu Argenté, Beige Sphinx, Beige Atlas, Bleu Uzès, Vert Cali, Beige Sloughi (Cottage), Beige Impala, Rouge Delage, Rouge Vallelunga, Bleu Romantique, Vert Chartreuse, Blanc Alaska (Entreprise only).

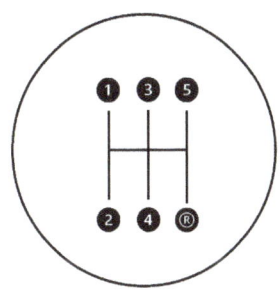

Gear change layout for five-speed manual GSA.

BX

The Visa and LN (described in the next chapter) were based on the existing Peugeot 104, but the BX, launched in Paris in October 1982, was the first all-new Citroën since the company's merger with Peugeot in 1976. The BX (originally codenamed 'Projet XB') was destined to replace the slightly smaller GSA, but the older car continued alongside it until 1986. It was initially planned as a five-door hatchback, with estate versions only arriving in 1985. Its styling, although finalised in-house, was primarily the work of Marcello Gandini at Bertone, who drew on his earlier designs for the Reliant/Anadol FW11 and the Volvo Tundra concept car. Several body panels, including the bonnet, tailgate and bumpers, were made from composite materials, resulting in a useful reduction in weight. Inside, the BX was still recognisably a Citroën, with the distinctive control pods and futuristic instruments already seen on the CX and GSA. Like the CX, the BX had a single windscreen wiper.

(Courtesy Citroën Communication)

Mechanically, however, the BX was clearly a product of the PSA Group. It still had Citroën's famed hydropneumatic suspension and all-round disc brakes, but shared its engines – all now water-cooled – and transmissions with other models from Peugeot. Reflecting the changing European market, diesel versions were introduced in 1983. Higher-performance

(Courtesy Citroën Communication)

124

BX

(Courtesy Citroën Communication/ Georges Guyot)

models followed in 1984 and 1985, when Citroën decided to enter the World Rally Championship with the four-wheel drive BX 4 TC. In 1986, the BX was facelifted: the Series 2 cars received a more conventional dashboard, while 16-valve engines and four-wheel drive versions were subsequently added to the range.

Series 1

The BX launched with two petrol engines: a 1360cc unit developing 62bhp (DIN) in the base model or 72bhp (DIN) in the BX 14 E and RE, and a 1580cc unit producing 90bhp (DIN) in the 16 RS and TRS. While the smaller engine had already seen service in the Peugeot 104, Citroën Visa and Talbot Samba, the larger XU5 engine – a modern, all-alloy design – made its début in the BX before being adopted by Peugeot. To meet local market requirements in Italy, Greece and Portugal, the smaller 1124cc engine from the Peugeot 104 was available in the BX 11. A version badged as the BX 15 was also sold in some countries: this had a de-tuned 1580cc engine with a single-choke carburettor, developing 80bhp (DIN).

RE/RS and TRS models could be recognised externally by their side rubbing strips, while the top-of-the-range 16 TRS had smoked polycarbonate windows set into its rear quarter

Base model brilliance. (Courtesy Citroën Communication)

125

panels. The TRS had the most generous level of equipment, with central locking, front electric windows, rear wash/wipe, front head restraints and a rev counter (presented as a bar graph) as standard. Alloy wheels, rear electric windows, tinted glass and a hifi pack could be ordered as options; air-conditioning was added to the options list in December 1983.

To begin with, the BX was built at Rennes-la-Janais in Brittany, then, in April 1983, production for the Spanish market started at Vigo. That summer, the 1984 model year saw the first changes to the BX. Power of the BX 16 engine increased to 92.5bhp (DIN), the gear change was made easier to use and conventionally-sized Michelins replaced the TRX tyres fitted to the 16 RS/TRS at launch.

An electrically operated glass sunroof became an option on the 14 RE, 16 RS and 16 TRS; wool blend tweed upholstery could also be specified on the 16 TRS. The most important development, however, was the introduction of the BX 19 D and 19 TRD diesel models, powered by the naturally aspirated 1.9-litre (1905cc) XUD9 engine which had been introduced on the Talbot Horizon and Peugeot 305. To compensate for the extra weight of the diesel engine, power-assisted steering was optional, and in February 1984 it became an option on the petrol-engined BX 16 too.

In March 1984, Citroën announced three Entreprise models for business users, available in 14 E, 16 RS and 19 D versions. To save tax they had only two seats and the rear doors were welded shut; the

BX 16 RS. (Courtesy Citroën Communication/Georges Guyot)

BX 16 TRS. (Courtesy Citroën Communication)

BX

(Courtesy Citroën Communication)

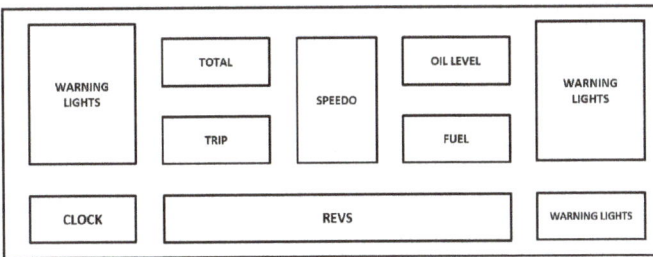

BX 16 TRS dashboard arrangement.

modifications were carried out by Gruau at Laval. Four months later, in July 1984, Citroën extended the BX range upwards, with the introduction of the 19 GT. The GT's 1905cc petrol engine, also fitted to the Peugeot 305 GTX, developed 105bhp (DIN) and was paired with a close-ratio five-speed manual gearbox. The GT's suspension was stiffer than on the other models in the BX range, but still offered a comfortable ride. The new version had front foglamps, rubbing strips on the bumpers, a rear spoiler and a new design of wheel trim. Power steering, tweed upholstery and a 14-function trip computer were standard. For the first time on the BX, the dashboard had conventional round dials, including a rev counter. At the same time, the standard dashboard on other BX models was slightly modified and now had a two-tone finish. Power and torque of the BX 16 engine increased slightly to 94bhp (DIN) and a ZF four-speed automatic transmission became optional on the 1.6-litre models. From December 1985, it could also be specified as an option on the 19 TRD.

In January 1985, Citroën presented the Leader special edition, based on the BX 14 E. Like the CX Leader introduced the previous year, it had distinctive metallic grey (Gris Perlé) paint with darker lower body panels, large plastic wheel trims and tartan cloth seats. Thanks to its keen pricing, the first run of 2500 cars sold out and the operation was repeated in autumn 1985, when 5000 more cars were built. In April 1986, a further 2300 examples of the 62bhp 1.4-litre BX Leader were produced, together with 800 Leader S saloons and 500 Leader S estates with the 1.6-litre petrol engine and 1400 examples of the diesel-powered Leader D. This time, in addition to metallic grey, metallic blue (Bleu Romantique) was also available, but was rarely specified.

The 19 GT was the starting point for the second limited-edition BX, the Digit, presented in September 1985. As its name suggested,

BX Leader interior. (Courtesy Citromuseum/Henri Fradet)

this had digital instruments, together with a trip computer at the base of the centre console, remote central locking and an elaborate Pioneer audio system with five speakers. Front and rear electric windows and central locking were standard, and it was available in a choice of three metallic colours: Gris Perlé, Gris Renard and Bleu Romantique. 4000 cars were built.

Following a proposal made by the coachbuilder Heuliez to design and build an estate model, the BX Break (also known as the Evasion) was announced in July 1985 for the 1986 model year. The estate body was only slightly longer and higher than the saloon and three versions were offered: the 16 RS and 19 TRS with petrol engines and the 19 RD diesel. The rear suspension was modified to carry heavier loads. The five-door estate body served as the basis for the new Entreprise models announced in February 1986: the 14 E (with the 72bhp 1360cc engine), 16 S and 19 D. Heuliez also produced small numbers of the luxurious Buffalo Break, based on the standard estate, a high-roof ambulance conversion and two three-door models, the Dyana estate and the Service van. Further market-specific van models were produced in Ireland (with no rear doors or side windows) and in Finland (with a high-top fibreglass roof).

For 1986, there were some changes to the 19 GT saloon: velour upholstery with a chevron motif replaced the tweed trim, there were new double chevron stickers in place of the 'GT' logo on the bonnet, and the trip computer became an extra-cost option.

(Courtesy Citroën Communication)

BX 14/E/RE

NUMBER PRODUCED: All BX models throughout career: 2,135,332 (saloon); 180,407 (estate); 14,857 (Entreprise saloon); 6420 (Entreprise estate).
PRICE AT LAUNCH: 48,900FF (BX).
ENGINE: Water-cooled, in-line four-cylinder petrol, SOHC design. Bore 75mm, stroke 77mm, capacity 1360cc, maximum power 72bhp (DIN) at 5750rpm (base model: 62bhp (DIN) at 5500rpm), Solex 32/34 twin-choke carburettor (base: Solex 30/30).
TRANSMISSION: Front-wheel drive, five-speed manual gearbox (base: four-speed) with synchromesh on all gears, floor-mounted gearlever. Final drive ratio: 3.867:1; gear ratios: first 3.87:1; second 2.30:1; third 1.52:1; fourth 1.12:1; fifth 0.91:1 (base: first 3.87:1; second 2.07:1; third 1.38:1; fourth 0.94:1).
BRAKES: Front and rear discs. Hydraulic servo control and dual circuits.
TYRES: 145 SR 14.
SUSPENSION: Fully independent, self-levelling hydropneumatic with anti-squat geometry and front and rear anti-roll bars. Front: struts; rear: trailing arms.
STEERING: Rack and pinion.
DIMENSIONS: Length: 4.23m (166.5in); width: 1.65m (65.0in); height: 1.36m (53.5in); wheelbase: 2.65m (104.5in); turning circle (between kerbs): 10.2m (33.5ft).
KERB WEIGHT: 900kg/1984lb (base: 885kg/1951lb).
CAPACITIES: Fuel: 44l (9.7gal); boot: 0.44m³ (15.7ft³).

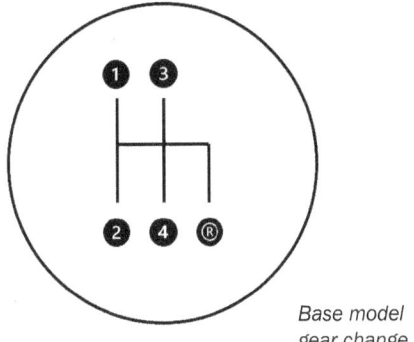

Base model gear change.

BX 16 RS/TRS

KEY DIFFERENCES
PRICE AT LAUNCH: 59,800FF (16 TRS).
ENGINE: Bore 83mm, stroke 73mm, capacity 1580cc, maximum power 90bhp (DIN) at 6000rpm (92.5bhp from 07/1983; 94bhp from 07/1984), Solex or Weber 32/34 twin-choke carburettor.
TRANSMISSION: Five-speed manual gearbox with synchromesh on all gears. Final drive ratio: 4.1875:1; gear ratios: first 3.31:1; second 1.88:1; third 1.28:1; fourth 0.97:1; fifth 0.76:1. ZF four-speed automatic optional from 07/1984.
TYRES: Michelin TRX 170/65 R 365 until 07/1983, then 165/70 R 14.
STEERING: Rack and pinion, power assistance optional from 02/1984.
KERB WEIGHT: 950kg (2094lb).
CAPACITIES: Fuel: 52l (11.4gal).

So-called 'chandelier' gear change on 16 RS/TRS.

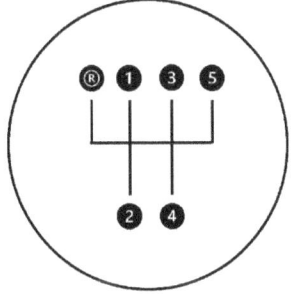

BX 19 RD Estate

KEY DIFFERENCES
ENGINE: Water-cooled, in-line four-cylinder diesel. Bore 83mm, stroke 88mm, capacity 1905cc, maximum power 65bhp (DIN) at 4600rpm, Roto-Diesel or Bosch injection.
TRANSMISSION: Five-speed manual gearbox with synchromesh on all gears, floor-mounted gearlever. Final drive ratio: 3.9375:1; gear ratios as 16 RS/TRS.
TYRES: 165/70 R 14.
STEERING: Rack and pinion, power assistance optional.
DIMENSIONS: Length: 4.40m (173.2in); width: 1.66m (65.4in); height: 1.43m (56.3in); wheelbase: 2.65m (104.5in); turning circle (between kerbs): 10.4m (34.1ft).

KERB WEIGHT: 1061kg (2339lb).
CAPACITIES: Fuel: 52l (11.4gal); boot (all seats folded): 1.8m^3 (63.7ft^3).

COLOURS (All models):
1983 Blanc Meije, Beige Colorado, Bleu Lagune, Rouge Vallelunga, Jaune Cédrat, Vert Tuileries, Noir, Beige Sloughi, Bleu Argenté, Gris Perlé, Gris Neptune.
1984 Blanc Meije, Beige Colorado, Bleu Camargue, Rouge Vallelunga, Rouge Delage, Noir, Beige Sloughi, Bleu Romantique, Gris Perlé, Gris Neptune.
1985 Beige Impala, Blanc Crémant, Blanc Meije, Rouge Delage, Rouge Vallelunga, Noir, Beige Sphinx, Bleu Navy, Bleu Romantique, Gris Perlé, Gris Renard, Vert Cali.
1986 Blanc Crémant, Blanc Meije, Bleu Iris, Rouge Delage, Rouge Vallelunga, Noir, Beige Sphinx, Bleu Romantique, Gris Perlé, Gris Renard, Vert Cali.

BX Sport

The high-performance BX Sport was introduced in March 1985 as a limited-edition model with a first run of 2500 cars, but its success led to it joining the permanent range in July that year. All the cars had left-hand drive and the model was not imported into the UK. Compared to the standard saloons, it had a very distinctive appearance. A unique bodykit was fitted, with body-coloured bumpers, a front spoiler with integrated foglamps, front wheelarch extensions, Gandini-style cutaway rear wheelarches, side sills and a rear spoiler. The interior was predominantly black, with velour-trimmed bucket seats taken from the CX GTi Turbo, a three-spoke sports steering wheel and the instrument pack from the BX 19 GT (with the addition of an oil pressure gauge). Standard equipment included power steering, central locking, tinted glass, front electric windows and rear wash/wipe.

Mechanically too, the Sport was extensively modified (by the renowned tuner Danielson): the 1.9-litre XU9 engine from the BX 19 GT received a new cylinder head, bigger valves and special pistons. The Sport had a new design of alloy wheel (later available on the BX 19 GTi) and wider, low-profile tyres, complementing its uprated suspension.

KEY DIFFERENCES
NUMBER PRODUCED: 7500.
PRICE AT LAUNCH: 104,500FF.
ENGINE: Bore 83mm, stroke 88mm, capacity 1905cc, maximum power 126bhp (DIN) at 5500-6000rpm, two Solex twin-choke C40 carburettors.
TRANSMISSION: Short-ratio five-speed manual gearbox with synchromesh on all gears.
TYRES: 185/60 R 14.
STEERING: Rack and pinion, with hydraulic power assistance.

BX

DIMENSIONS: Length: 4.22m (166.1in); width: 1.67m (65.7in); height: 1.35m (53.1in).
KERB WEIGHT: 1010kg (2227lb).
COLOURS: Gris Renard, Gris Perlé, Rouge Vallelunga, Blanc Meije (from 1986 MY), Noir Verni (from 1986 MY).

BX 4 TC

In 1985, Citroën took the BX as its starting point to enter Group B in the World Rally Championship. The BX 4 TC had four-wheel drive, like the Audi Quattro, and retained the standard car's hydropneumatic suspension and power steering. The four-cylinder in-line engine, based on that of the Peugeot 505 Turbo, was boosted by a Garrett turbocharger and installed longitudinally, rather than transversely as in the standard BX. This required the front of the car to be redesigned with a longer bonnet and a colossal front overhang. Its five-speed gearbox came from the SM. In competition spec, it developed a heady 360bhp, giving it a top speed of 280km/h (174mph). Heuliez built 20 cars for rallying, but the model competed in just three rounds of the WRC before Group B was abolished at the end of 1986. It suffered from reliability problems and its only result was a sixth-place finish on the Swedish Rally.

To homologate the car in Group B, the FIA stipulated that 200 roadgoing versions of the rally car had to be built. Also produced by Heuliez, they were fitted with a bodykit and huge wheelarch extensions. All the cars were finished in white (Blanc Meije) with blue and red stripes. The wheels and brakes were supplied by the CX 25 GTi Turbo, while the seats and rear spoiler came from the BX Sport. The cars were marketed through Citroën's dealer network, but only 86 of the 200 cars built found takers and the unsold examples were scrapped. Its rarity

BX 4 TC stands between DS and ZX.

Citroën Cars 1934 to 1986 – A Pictorial History

Bertone's Zabrus design study.

makes it highly sought after by collectors today. The 4 TC was also the basis for a design study by Bertone, the four-seat Zabrus coupé. This never went into production, but some elements of its design were picked up in the XM in 1989.

KEY DIFFERENCES
NUMBER PRODUCED: 86 (road).
PRICE AT LAUNCH: 248,500FF.
ENGINE: Water-cooled, four-cylinder petrol, SOHC design. Bore 91.4mm, stroke 81.6mm, capacity 2141cc, maximum power 200bhp (DIN) at 5250rpm, Bosch K-Jetronic fuel-injection. Garrett turbocharger and air-to-air intercooler.
TRANSMISSION: Four-wheel drive, five-speed manual gearbox with synchromesh on all gears, floor-mounted gearlever.
BRAKES: ventilated discs at front and rear. Hydraulic servo control and dual circuits.
TYRES: Michelin TRX 210/55 VR 390.
SUSPENSION: Fully independent, self-levelling hydropneumatic.
STEERING: Rack and pinion, with hydraulic power assistance.
DIMENSIONS: Length: 4.51m (177.6in); width: 1.83m (72.0in); wheelbase: 2.61m (102.8in).
KERB WEIGHT: 1280kg (2822lb).

Series 2

In July 1986, just four years after its launch, the BX underwent a substantial midlife facelift, carried out by Citroën's in-house designer Carl Olsen. Externally, the bumpers were more rounded (although the estate kept the pre-facelift rear bumper), the wings were widened and there were new door mirrors and front indicators with clear lenses. The most noticeable change was inside the car, where the original dashboard with its satellite controls was replaced by a more orthodox instrument panel with traditional column stalks.

Several new models were added to the

Series 2 interior, here in 1991 GTi auto. (Courtesy Citroën Communication)

BX 16 Soupapes.

range. The BX D was a lower-powered entry-level diesel, with a smaller 1769cc engine producing 60bhp (DIN). The BX 16 S meanwhile made it possible to order the 1580cc petrol engine with the most basic trim. On the BX 19 GTi, electronic fuel-injection replaced the carburettor set-up of the 19 GT and power increased to 125bhp (DIN). The GTi was more overtly sporting in appearance than the GT, with a rear spoiler and new bucket-style seats; alloy wheels like those fitted to the BX Sport were optional, as were ABS brakes. The carburettor-engined 19 GT made way for the BX 19 TRS: this could be ordered with either manual or automatic transmission, the latter making for a relaxing long-distance car (as the author's father found over several contented years of BX ownership). There were smaller improvements to trim and equipment across the range and black leather upholstery became an option on the TRS and GTi models.

In July 1987, the GTi 16 Soupapes arrived as the new performance flagship of the BX range, with a 16-valve 1.9-litre engine producing 160bhp (DIN). In March 1988, saloon and estate versions of the BX turbodiesel went on sale. In 1989, the BX GTi 16 Soupapes was fitted with a more aggressive bodykit and became simply the BX 16 Soupapes. The same year, four-wheel drive became available, first on TRi-spec saloon and estate models and then on the 19 GTi 4x4, which benefitted from standard-fit ABS and a Torsen-type limited-slip differential.

The BX received a further mild facelift in October 1989, when the previous R and TR trim levels were renamed TG and TZ. A number of special editions – the Olympique, Image, Tonic, Calanque, Millésime and Cottage – helped sustain interest in the now ageing BX. In 1991, the range was simplified after the smaller ZX was introduced. Production of the saloons came to an end in December 1993 and of the estates in July 1994 as the Xantia took their place.

BX 4x4 saloon.

Other models from the 1970s and 1980s

The second half of the 1970s and the 1980s were a period of transition for Citroën as it came under Peugeot's control, and this can be clearly seen in the cars from this era. The LN and Visa were the last to be powered by the legendary flat-twin engine which originated in the first 2CV in 1948. Increasingly, Citroën's small cars from this period were based on Peugeot's platforms and used its water-cooled four-cylinder engines. The facelifted Visa II, launched in 1981, was more conventional than the first series and sold all the better for it. The Axel, the final car described here, was the last Citroën to be designed without any input from Peugeot.

LNA. (Courtesy Citroën Communication/ Laurent Lacoste)

Visa 11 E. (Courtesy Citroën Communication/ Georges Guyot)

Axel 11 R.

Citroën LN and LNA

In 1972, Citroën's R&D department began work on 'Projet TA,' a new model to replace the Ami, which would be powered by either the flat-twin from the A-Series or the flat-four from the GS. When Peugeot bailed out

Citroën at the end of 1974, however, the programme was reviewed to save costs. The revised 'Projet VD' – for 'Voiture Diminuée' (compact car) – was based on the Peugeot 104 platform and led to two new Citroëns: the hastily developed three-door LN city car and the five-door Visa hatchback.

134

Other models from the 1970s and 1980s

The LN – pronounced Hélène in French – was named after the Greek goddess Helena, following the tradition inaugurated by the DS in 1955. It was built on the chassis of the short-wheelbase Peugeot 104 Z, and used the same three-door coupé bodyshell with few changes. Externally, the air vents in the rear quarter pillars were deleted and the Dyane's rectangular chrome headlamp trims fitted. Citroën had planned to use torsion bar suspension, but this made way for the MacPherson struts and trailing arms used on the 104. Only the engine – the 602cc flat-twin from the Ami 8, developing 32bhp (DIN) – and the gearbox, albeit now with a floor change, were 'proper' Citroën items. The dashboard came straight from the 104, but the single-spoke steering wheel was a nod towards Citroën's other models. The company's traditional customers were aghast, seeing in the new model a betrayal of Peugeot's assurances that it would retain the marque's individual identity.

Presented at the Paris Motor Show in October 1976, the LN was simply equipped but cheap to buy and run. It was practical too: the LN was the first French car with a split-folding rear seat as standard. A centrifugal clutch was available as an option. In 1977, a tax-saving Service version for business users was added: this kept the saloon's rear windows, but had only two seats. There were no other significant changes to the LN, however, as in November 1978, Citroën introduced the better finished and more powerful LNA. The LN had been built only with left-hand drive and sold mainly in France and its neighbouring countries, but the LNA was marketed more widely throughout Europe.

1979 LNA. (Courtesy Citroën Communication/ Georges Guyot)

1980 LNA interior. (Courtesy Peter Singhof – Artcurial Motorcars)

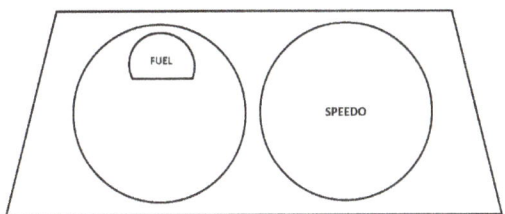

Citroën Cars 1934 to 1986 – A Pictorial History

The letter 'A' in the LNA's name stood for 'Athlétique' (Athletic). The new model was fitted with the final iteration of the flat-twin engine, as used in the newly introduced Visa. Bored out to 652cc, it produced 36bhp (DIN) and had electronic ignition. The centrifugal clutch was no longer offered. Externally, the LNA could be recognised by its small chrome hubcaps and black side rubbing strips, while inside, carpets were now fitted as standard. An Entreprise version for business users was again available. The LN briefly continued on sale alongside the LNA but was discontinued in 1979.

Two independent French coachbuilders produced convertibles based on the LNA, the LM Sovra LM5 and the Bertin-Cholet Marina. Only a handful of each were built, their sales handicapped not least by the competition they faced from the very similar Talbot Samba Cabrio, produced by Pininfarina.

There were minor modifications to the LNA's upholstery and equipment in 1980-1982. In October 1981, Citroën introduced the short-lived Club model featuring metallic paint, beige cloth upholstery (with reclining front seats), a radio aerial and optional rear wash/wipe. The biggest changes came in July 1982, for the 1983 model year, with the launch of the new 11 E and better equipped 11 RE models. Effectively rebadged Peugeots, these were fitted with the 1124cc four-cylinder engine from the Peugeot 104, sometimes called the 'Suitcase' engine. The basic two-cylinder LNA continued, but with a revised 652 'ECO' engine for improved economy. At the same time, the LNA received black plastic bumpers, larger rear lights and new wheels and exterior trim. Inside, a parcel shelf was now fitted and electric windows were optional on the 11 RE. Right-hand drive versions of the revised LNA were introduced in the UK at the start of 1983, but they sold poorly and were discontinued after only two years. Two special editions of the LNA were sold in France in 1983: the white Prisu (600 cars), produced in association with the supermarket chain Prisunic, and the 11 E Cannelle (2000 cars), which sported metallic paint, alloy wheels and tweed upholstery. Outside France, there were limited editions in Austria (the Elysée), the UK (the Inca) and Italy (the Pepita). A lower-spec 10 E model with a 954cc version of the Peugeot four-pot developing 45bhp was also sold in Italy in 1985, but only 248 were produced.

There were further minor changes to the LNA in July 1985 and the 11 RE was replaced by the 11 RS with shorter gearing for better acceleration. Production of all LNA models ended in the summer of 1986, shortly before the AX was introduced.

The limited-edition LNA 11 E Cannelle.

Above and right:
The Bertin-Cholet Marina convertible.

Other models from the 1970s and 1980s

LN

NUMBER PRODUCED: 116,931 (saloon); 12,680 (Service).
PRICE AT LAUNCH: 17,500FF.
ENGINE: Air-cooled, two-cylinder (flat-twin) petrol, OHV layout. Bore 74mm, stroke 70mm, capacity 602cc, maximum power 32bhp (DIN) at 5750rpm, Solex 26/35 twin-choke carburettor.
TRANSMISSION: Front-wheel drive, four-speed manual gearbox with synchromesh on all gears, floor-mounted gearlever. Final drive ratio: 4.375:1; gear ratios: first 4.55:1; second 2.50:1; third 1.81:1; fourth 1.15:1. Optional centrifugal clutch.
BRAKES: Front: discs; rear: drums. Dual circuits.
TYRES: 135 SR 13.
SUSPENSION: All-independent. Front: MacPherson-type with coil springs, telescopic shock absorbers and anti-roll bar; rear: trailing arms, coil springs and telescopic shock absorbers.
STEERING: Rack and pinion.
DIMENSIONS: Length: 3.38m (133.1in); width: 1.52m (59.8in); height: 1.37m (53.9in); wheelbase: 2.23m (87.8in); turning circle (between kerbs): 9.4m (30.8ft).
KERB WEIGHT: 706kg (1556lb).
CAPACITIES: Fuel: 40l (8.8gal); boot: 0.12m^3 (4.2ft^3).
COLOURS: Beige Gazelle, Bleu Myosotis, Rouge Soleil, Bleu Centaurée, Vert Papyrus.

LNA

KEY DIFFERENCES
NUMBER PRODUCED: 164,275 (saloon); 59,497 (Entreprise).
ENGINE: Air-cooled, two-cylinder (flat-twin) petrol, OHV layout. Bore 77mm, stroke 70mm, capacity 652cc, maximum power 36bhp (DIN) at 5500rpm (34.5bhp from 07/1982), Solex 26/35 twin-choke carburettor.
TRANSMISSION: Front-wheel drive, four-speed manual gearbox with synchromesh on all gears, floor-mounted gearlever. Final drive ratio: 4.125:1 (3.89:1 from 07/1982); gear ratios: first 4.55:1; second 2.50:1; third 1.64:1; fourth 1.15:1.
DIMENSIONS: Length: 3.40m/133.9in (3.43m/134.9in from 07/1982).
KERB WEIGHT: 710kg (1565lb).

LNA 11 E/RE

KEY DIFFERENCES
ENGINE: Water-cooled, in-line four-cylinder petrol, transversely mounted, SOHC design. Bore 72mm, stroke 69mm, capacity 1124cc, maximum power 50bhp (DIN) at 5500rpm, Solex 32 PBIS carburettor.
TRANSMISSION: Front-wheel drive, four-speed manual gearbox with synchromesh on all gears, floor-mounted gearlever. Final drive ratio: 3.176:1 (11 RS: 3.563:1); gear ratios: first 3.88:1; second 2.07:1; third 1.38:1; fourth 0.94:1.
DIMENSIONS: Length: 3.43m (134.9in).
KERB WEIGHT: 749kg (1651lb).

COLOURS (All models 1983): Beige Colorado, Blanc Meije, Bleu Argenté, Bleu Nuit, Noir, Rouge de Garance, Sable Doré, Vert Tourmaline.

Citroën Visa

Based on the platform from the Peugeot 104, the Visa was introduced at the Paris Motor Show in October 1978. The successor to the Ami 8, it was positioned between the cheaper and simpler 2CV and Dyane, and the more sophisticated GS. Citroën emphasised its versatility and its compact yet spacious five-door hatchback body. The exterior styling was conventional compared with several of its predecessors, although the first-series cars had impact-absorbent bumpers giving the front of the car an unfortunate snout-like appearance. Inside, however, the Visa kept Citroën's traditional single-spoke steering wheel and PRN satellite controls. As Michael Scarlett, the technical editor of *Autocar*, was moved to write: "You can't keep a Citroën draughtsman down when it comes to ideas about control ergonomics."

The Visa launched with three models, powered by two different engines. The Spécial and Club used the 652cc version of the air-cooled flat-twin as fitted to the new LNA. The Super had Peugeot's 1.1-litre four-cylinder

137

engine from the 104, an all-aluminium overhead cam unit, with the gearbox in the sump. Both engines were paired exclusively with four-speed manual gearboxes; automatic transmission was never available on the Visa. The suspension also came from Peugeot, using MacPherson struts at the front and trailing arms with coil springs at the rear, but was re-tuned to give a softer ride.

All models came with inertia-reel seatbelts, two-speed windscreen wipers and a heated rear window as standard. The Club and Super models were better equipped, with a clock, rear parcel shelf, reclining seats, reversing and rear fog lights, chrome strips on the radiator grille and wheel trims all included. In addition, the Super had halogen headlamps, side rubbing strips, carpets, a dipping rear-view mirror and cloth-trimmed dashboard. The seats were in a mix of jersey (cloth) and vinyl on the Spécial and Club, and fully trimmed in jersey with a polka dot pattern on the Super. Factory options on all models included metallic paint, a rear wash/wipe and tinted glass; front head restraints were a dealer-fit option on the Club and Super.

There were minor changes to the Visa in July 1979, but in July 1980 the original Super model was replaced by two new versions. The economical Super E kept the 1124cc engine with a new Solex carburettor and slightly longer gear ratios. The performance-oriented Super X was equipped with larger anti-roll bars and uprated brakes, while the engine was bored out to 1219cc and developed 64bhp (DIN) at 6000rpm.

Visa Spécial/Club

NUMBER PRODUCED: 1,254,390 (all models).
ENGINE: Air-cooled, two-cylinder (flat-twin) petrol, OHV layout, installed longitudinally. Bore 77mm, stroke 70mm, capacity 652cc, maximum power 36bhp (DIN) at 5500rpm, Solex 26/35 twin-choke carburettor.
TRANSMISSION: Front-wheel drive, four-speed manual gearbox with synchromesh on all gears, floor-mounted gearlever. Final drive ratio: 4.125:1; gear ratios: first 4.54:1; second 2.50:1; third 1.64:1; fourth 1.14:1.
BRAKES: Front: discs; rear: drums. Hydraulic servo control and dual circuits.
TYRES: 135 SR 13.

First-generation Visa Super.

Other models from the 1970s and 1980s

SUSPENSION: All-independent. Front: MacPherson-type with coil springs, telescopic shock absorbers and anti-roll bar; rear: trailing arms, coil springs and telescopic shock absorbers.
STEERING: Rack and pinion.
DIMENSIONS: Length: 3.69m (145.3in); width: 1.51m (59.4in); height: 1.41m (55.4in); wheelbase: 2.43m (95.7in); turning circle (between kerbs): 9.3m (30.5ft).
KERB WEIGHT: 735kg (1620lb).
CAPACITIES: Fuel: 40l (8.8gal); boot: 0.30m³/10.6ft³ (Club: 0.28m³/9.9ft³).

Visa II Club.

Visa Super

KEY DIFFERENCES
ENGINE: Water-cooled, four-cylinder petrol, SOHC design, transversely mounted. Bore 72mm, stroke 69mm, capacity 1124cc, maximum power 57bhp (DIN) at 6250rpm, Solex 32 PBIS twin-choke carburettor.
TRANSMISSION: Final drive ratio: 3.5625:1; gear ratios: first 3.88:1; second 2.29:1; third 1.50:1; fourth 1.04:1.
TYRES: 145 SR 13.
DIMENSIONS: width: 1.53m (60.4in); height: 1.42m (55.7in); wheelbase: 2.42m (95.3in); turning circle (between kerbs): 9.5m (31.0ft).
KERB WEIGHT: 800kg (1764lb).
CAPACITIES: as Club.

Interior of the Visa 11 E. (Courtesy Citroën Communication/Georges Guyot)

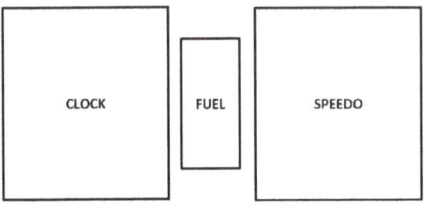

COLOURS (All models 1978): Beige Nevada, Bleu Myosotis, Brun Vésuve (Super only), Jaune Mimosa, Rouge Géranium, Vert Reinette, Bleu Régate, Gris Nacré.

Visa II

Despite the changes made in 1980, sales of the Visa were disappointing, with strong competition from the Renault 5, available as a five-door from 1979. In March 1981, Citroën therefore launched the revised Visa II, adroitly but inexpensively restyled by Heuliez. The updated models had new bumpers with a more orthodox front grille, side rubbing strips, new taillights and black window surrounds. The model range was unchanged, but the options now included alloy wheels, a panoramic sunroof and front fog lamps. Soon afterwards, in July 1981, a five-speed gearbox became available on the Super X. For 1982, Citroën introduced the basic 'L' model with equipment similar to the Spécial. It had either the regular 1124cc engine or a smaller 954cc engine for tax reasons in markets such as Greece, but sold poorly.

COLOURS (All models 1981): Beige Daim, Beige Colorado, Blanc Meije, Bleu Azurite, Bleu Régate, Rouge Géranium, Cuivre Tammela, Vert Tamaris, Noir.

The facelift operation as a whole proved highly successful, with sales increasing by more than 50%, and allowed the Visa to keep going until 1988, when it was effectively replaced by the five-door AX. During the 1980s, Citroën extended the Visa range with more powerful and luxurious versions. The 1983 model year saw the arrival of two new models: the Super E GL with improved equipment and a removable two-piece rear seat, and the more powerful Visa GT to replace the Super X. The GT had a 1360cc engine with twin downdraught Weber carburettors producing 80bhp (DIN), mated to a five-speed gearbox, as well as sporty exterior styling with alloy wheels (shod with Michelin TRX tyres), a front air dam and rear spoiler. It was available in Gris Perlé, Noir and Rouge Vallelunga.

For 1984, Citroën returned to Heuliez to produce a four-door convertible based on the Visa Super E/11 RE, the Décapotable. This kept the doors and window frames unchanged from the hatchback.

The big news in 1984, however, was the introduction of the diesel-powered 17 D and 17 RD, which shared their 1769cc XUD engine (here delivering 60bhp) and transmission with the Peugeot 205. The new naming convention was also applied to the petrol-engined 11 E

(Courtesy Citroën Communication/Georges Guyot)

(replacing the L) and 11 RE (superseding the Super E), while the Spécial was now known simply as 'Visa.' A year later, at the Paris Motor Show in October 1984, Citroën added the 14 TRS as the luxury model in the range. It was powered by the 1360cc petrol engine, but in milder (60bhp) tune than in the GT. The 14

Visa 14 TRS next to limited-edition Platine.

Other models from the 1970s and 1980s

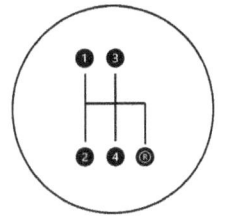
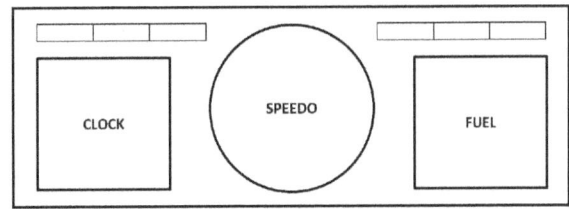

Dashboard and gear change layout for the Visa 11 E/RE.

TRS, like all the regular models in the Visa range, received a new design of dashboard with conventional instruments and column stalks.

The GT was itself succeeded for the 1985 model year by the GTI, now fitted with the same fuel-injected 1.6-litre engine as the Peugeot 205 GTi. It could be recognised by its plastic wheelarch extensions, twin headlamps, alloy wheels and round instruments. Electric windows, tinted glass, central locking and a sunroof could be specified as extras. The GTI's chassis and performance were praised, but it was criticised for its lack of refinement and small boot.

Visa GTI

KEY DIFFERENCES

ENGINE: Water-cooled, four-cylinder petrol, SOHC design. Bore 83mm, stroke 73mm, capacity 1580cc, maximum power 105bhp (DIN) at 6250rpm (115bhp from 07/1986), Bosch L-Jetronic fuel-injection.
TRANSMISSION: Five-speed manual gearbox with synchromesh on all gears, floor-mounted gearlever. Final drive ratio: 3.9375:1; gear ratios: first 3.31:1; second 1.88:1; third 1.36:1; fourth 1.07:1; fifth 0.87:1.

BRAKES: Front: ventilated discs; rear: drums. Hydraulic servo control and dual circuits.
TYRES: 185/60 R 13.
SUSPENSION: All-independent. Front: MacPherson-type with coil springs and telescopic shock absorbers; rear: trailing arms, coil springs and telescopic shock absorbers. Anti-roll bars at front and rear.
DIMENSIONS: Length: 3.73m (146.7in); width: 1.60m (63.0in); height: 1.37m (53.9in); wheelbase: 2.42m (95.3in).
KERB WEIGHT: 870kg (1918lb).
CAPACITIES: Fuel: 43l (9.5gal); boot: 0.26m^3 (9.2ft^3).
COLOURS: Blanc Crémant, Blanc Meije, Gris Perlé, Noir, Rouge Vallelunga.

There were fewer notable changes in the final part of the Visa's career, but for 1987, the 11 E was replaced in several markets by the 10 E with a smaller, 954cc four-cylinder engine.

Throughout the Visa's career, Citroën produced several limited editions of the Visa as outlined in the table below.

Individual markets offered additional special editions, such as the Champagne, Drapeau and Platinum models sold in the UK in 1982-83.

Year	Limited edition	Based on ...	Number produced
1979	Carte Noire	Visa Super	2500
1980	Sextant	Visa Super	2000
1982	West End	Visa second Super E	1800
1983	Platine	Visa 11 RE	2000
1984	Olympique	Visa 11 E	3000
1985	Challenger	Visa 11 E (with GT engine)	3500
1985	Tonic (14 S)	Visa GT and Chrono	2000
1985-1987	Leader	Visa 11 E and 17 D	11,800

Citroën Cars 1934 to 1986 – A Pictorial History

Limited edition Visas: the West-End and the Sextant (below).

Visa Chrono and 1000 Pistes

Citroën initially took the Visa rallying with a Group 5 (Prototype) version of the Super X. In December 1981, it developed a new Trophée version of the Group 5 car to be homologated in Group B. This adopted the 1219cc engine from the Super X but with a modified cylinder head and twin Weber 40 DCOE carburettors to deliver 100bhp (DIN). Lexan side windows and fibreglass body panels kept the weight down to under 700kg (1543lb). 200 cars were built and enjoyed considerable success in competition.

In March 1982, Citroën drew on the Trophée rally car to produce 1000 roadgoing Chrono models for the French market. Still based on the Visa II Super X, they were powered by a 93bhp (DIN) version of the 1360cc engine and had a blue, white and red colour scheme with front and rear spoilers, extended wheelarches and alloy wheels. The dashboard was modelled on the Trophée, with a full complement of Jaeger instruments. The operation was repeated in 1983, when 1600 Chronos were sold in other European markets in each country's national colours.

Other models from the 1970s and 1980s

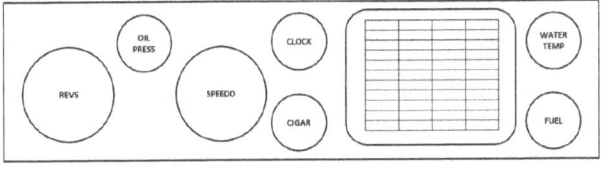

Above: French-market Visa Chrono.

Dashboard of the Chrono. (Courtesy Citroën Communication)

Below: Italian-market Chrono. (Courtesy Citroën Communication)

In November 1983, Citroën went a stage further with the four-wheel drive Visa 1000 Pistes. Built for rallying in Group B, 200 roadgoing cars were also produced for homologation purposes. These had a rear limited-slip diff and disc brakes all round, while the 1360cc engine was uprated to 112bhp (DIN). They can be recognised by their dual double chevron badges on the front grille and '4 Roues Motrices' (4WD) side stripes (see overleaf).

Citroën Cars 1934 to 1986 – A Pictorial History

*Visa 1000 Pistes.
(Courtesy Bonhams)*

Citroën C15

Citroën's first Visa-based offering for business users was an Entreprise version of the Visa second Spécial hatchback, with the rear doors welded shut, introduced for the 1983 model year. In October 1984, however, it launched the C15 van to replace the venerable Acadiane. This was built on a longer wheelbase than the Visa, and had rear suspension similar to the BX to provide a flat load floor. The single, side-opening rear door was soon replaced by twin rear doors for easier access in tight spaces. In addition to the standard van, Citroën also sold a version with rear side windows and a rear seat, a long-wheelbase model, a small number of pickups (built by Gruau) and a chassis-only model for conversions such as camper vans.

Late-model C15 in UK. (Courtesy Chris Hughes)

The C15 was initially available with either petrol or diesel engines (as the C15 E and C15 D respectively), although the petrol model was discontinued in the early 1990s. Both versions had noticeably better performance than the Acadiane and an increased payload of up to 765kg (1687lb). In the UK, the C15 was available in red or white, wittily promoted as 'Van Rouge' and 'Van Blanc.' Its career ran until 2005 and many C15s remain in use today.

NUMBER PRODUCED: 1,181,471 (all models).
ENGINE: Water-cooled, four-cylinder petrol

(Courtesy Chris Hughes)

Other models from the 1970s and 1980s

(Courtesy Chris Hughes)

UK brochure for C15. (Courtesy Citroën Communication)

(C15 E) or diesel (C15 D).
C15 E: Bore 72mm, stroke 69mm, capacity 1124cc, maximum power 47bhp (DIN) at 5750rpm. **C15 D:** Bore 80mm, stroke 88mm, capacity 1769cc, maximum power 60bhp (DIN) at 4600rpm.
TRANSMISSION: Front-wheel drive, four-speed manual gearbox with synchromesh on all gears, floor-mounted gearlever.
C15 E: Final drive ratio: 4.07:1; gear ratios: first 3.08:1; second 1.65:1; third 1.09:1; fourth 0.75:1.
C15 D: Final drive ratio: 3.8125:1; gear ratios: first 3.31:1; second 1.88:1; third 1.15:1; fourth 0.80:1.
BRAKES: Front: discs; rear: drums. Hydraulic servo control and dual circuits.
TYRES: C15 E: 145 R 13; **C15 D:** 155 R 13.
SUSPENSION: All-independent. Front: MacPherson-type with coil springs and telescopic shock absorbers; rear: trailing arms, coil springs and telescopic shock absorbers. Anti-roll bars at front and rear.
STEERING: Rack and pinion. Power assistance optional from 1993.
DIMENSIONS: Length: 3.99m (157.3in); width: 1.64m (64.4in); height: 1.80m (70.9in); wheelbase: 2.74m (107.9in); turning circle (between kerbs): **C15 E:** 10.0m (32.8ft); **C15 D:** 11.0m (36.2ft).
KERB WEIGHT: C15 E: 850kg (1874lb); **C15 D:** 945kg (2083lb).
CAPACITIES: Fuel: 47l (10.3gal); load space: 2.67m^3 (94.4ft^3).

Citroën Axel

When Peugeot took the decision to base Citroën's new small cars – the LN and Visa – on the platform of the 104, it seemed that 'Projet TA' had been consigned to history. In 1976, however, the PSA Group won a call to tender to set up a modern factory and build a new car in Romania. The abandoned project was dusted down and the design modified to cope with Romania's rough roads and harsh winters. At the end of 1976, the Oltcit joint venture (from the province of **Oltenia** + **Citroën**) was formed between Citroën and the Romanian government to build the new model. Production eventually got under way in 1981. Under the terms of the agreement, Oltcit sold the car – now christened the Axel – in the Communist Bloc, while PSA marketed it in Western Europe.

Whereas 'Projet TA' had originally been a four-door, the new model was a sturdily built three-door hatchback. It was powered by either the Visa's 652cc flat-twin (in the Spécial) or the 1129cc flat-four from the GS (in the 11 R and RL). Suspension was by torsion bars rather than the MacPherson struts favoured by Peugeot. The dashboard featured PRN satellite controls similar to those in the Visa and GSA.

In July 1984 Citroën rebadged the car as the Citroën Axel for sale in France, Austria, the Benelux and Italy, but it was never officially imported into the UK. Oltcit's two-cylinder Spécial was dropped, but three four-cylinder models were offered: base, 11 R and 12 TRS. The 11 R had halogen headlamps, rear wash/wipe, intermittent front wipe, front headrests, a rev counter and front and rear inertia-reel seatbelts as standard. Externally, it could be recognised by its plastic wheel trims and side rubbing strips. The 12 TRS was an addition to the range, with the 1299cc engine and five-speed manual gearbox from the GSA. Alloy wheels were standard and metallic paint the only option available. Alongside the three saloon versions, Citroën listed a pair of two-seat Entreprise models for business users: the 1129cc base model and the larger-engined 12 TRS Entreprise.

The Axel was keenly priced (the base model was cheaper even than the 2CV) but it was outdated in appearance and the 12 TRS was thirsty. Above all, it suffered from appalling build quality, resulting in significant warranty claims. Sales declined steadily after 1985 and production ended in 1988.

NUMBER PRODUCED: 47,009 (saloon); 13,175 (Entreprise).

Other models from the 1970s and 1980s

The Axel Entreprise.

PRICES AT LAUNCH: 37,000FF (base) – 45,200FF (12 TRS).
ENGINE: Air-cooled, four-cylinder (flat-four) petrol, SOHC design. Bore 74mm (12 TRS: 79.4mm), stroke 65.6mm, capacity 1129cc (12 TRS: 1299cc), maximum power 57bhp (DIN) at 6250rpm (12 TRS: 61bhp (DIN) at 5500rpm), Solex 28 CIT carburettor.
TRANSMISSION: Front-wheel drive, four-speed manual gearbox with synchromesh on all gears, floor-mounted gearlever. Final drive ratio: 4.125:1 (12 TRS: 3.89:1); gear ratios: first 3.82:1; second 2.29:1; third 1.50:1; fourth 1.03:1 (12 TRS: first 3.82:1; second 2.29:1; third 1.50:1; fourth 1.13:1; fifth 0.91:1).
BRAKES: Front: inboard discs; rear: discs. Hydraulic servo assistance and dual circuits.
TYRES: 145 SR 13 (12 TRS: 160/65 TR 340 TRX).
SUSPENSION: Front: double wishbones with longitudinal torsion bars; rear: trailing arms

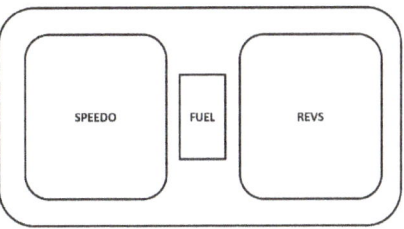

with transverse torsion bars.
STEERING: Rack and pinion.
DIMENSIONS: Length: 3.73m (146.7in); width: 1.54m (60.7in); height: 1.42m (55.8in); wheelbase: 2.37m (93.3in); turning circle (between kerbs): 9.1m (29.7ft).
KERB WEIGHT: 860kg/1896lb (12 TRS: 875kg/1929lb).
CAPACITIES: Fuel: 42l (9.2gal); boot: 0.30m^3/10.5ft^3 (Entreprise: 1.1m^3/38.9ft^3).
COLOURS (1986): Beige Atlas, Beige Sphinx, Blanc Meije, Bleu Romantique, Gris Perlé, Rouge Vallelunga.

More in the Pictorial History series:

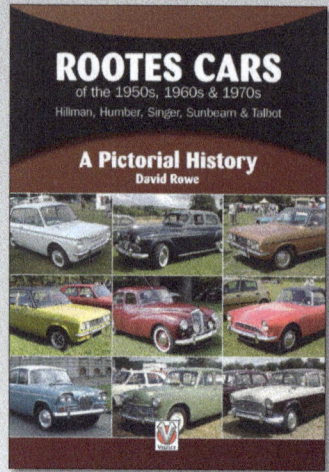

ISBN: 978-1-787114-43-2

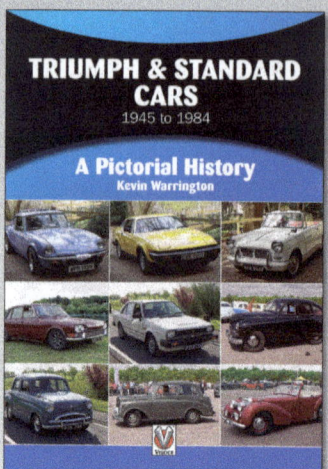

ISBN: 978-1-787110-77-9

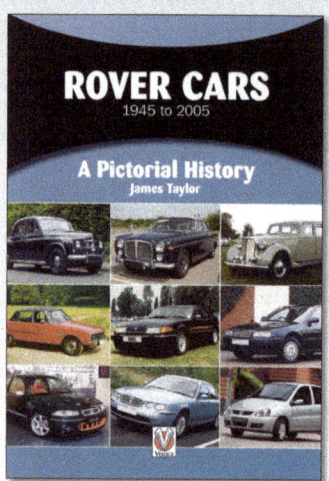

ISBN: 978-1-787116-09-2

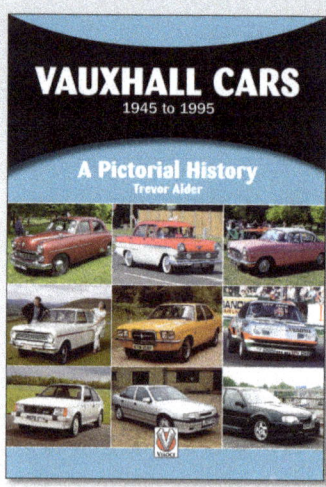

ISBN: 978-1-787115-93-4

The Pictorial History series provides the ultimate guide to these classic marques. Ideal for the enthusiast or collector, or for those who enjoy a trip down memory lane. The books cover every model of the period, are packed with full model specs, interesting facts, and fully illustrated in colour.

For more information and price details, visit our website at www.veloce.co.uk

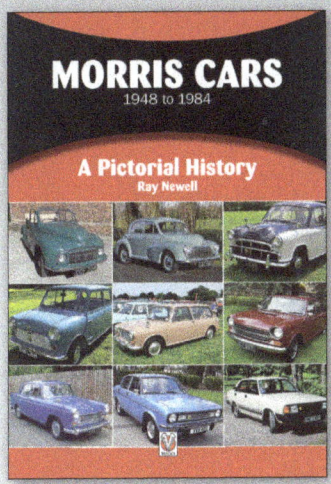

ISBN: 978-1-787110-55-7

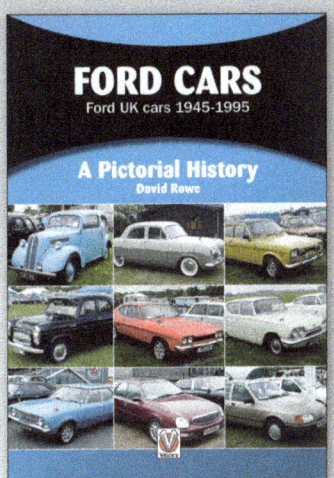

ISBN: 978-1-787116-42-9

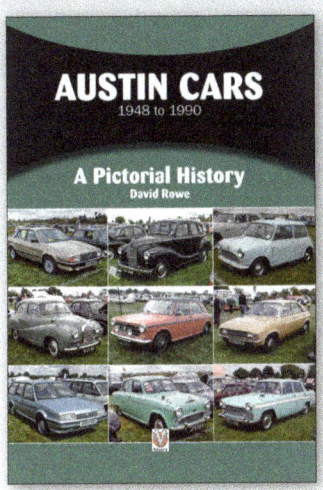

ISBN: 978-1-787112-19-3

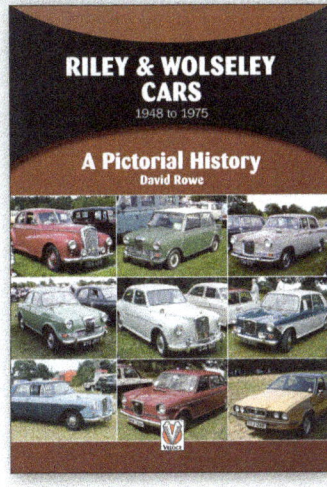

ISBN: 978-1-787117-91-4

These compact books are handy to take to a car show, and a great addition to any automotive library. As a collection they provide a comprehensive reference source.
See the full range on the Veloce website, more titles coming soon!

email info@veloce.co.uk/tel (+44) 01305 260068

More from Veloce:

A revealing insight into the work of a practically unknown aeronautic engineer who created the revolutionary front-wheel drive Traction Avant, the minimalist 2CV and the Citroën DS, a sensation in the automotive world in 1955, and still an icon of original automobile engineering and avant-garde design.

ISBN: 978-1-845842-44-4
Paperback • 23.8x17cm • 144 pages

For more information and price details, visit our website at www.veloce.co.uk

The definitive guide to restoring the Citroën 2CV and its close relatives the Dyane, Van, Ami 6 & Mehari. Aimed at the owner, here is a step-by-step, hands-on guide to every aspect of restoration including body, trim and mechanical components. Over 1400 colour photos illustrate every stage of the process.

ISBN: 978-1-903706-44-2
Paperback • 27x20.7cm • 272 pages

email info@veloce.co.uk/tel (+44) 01305 260068

INDEX

Model	Years of production	Pages
2CV	1948-1990	72-96
4x4 Sahara	1958-1971	85
Fourgonnette (van)	1950-1978	91
UK-built cars	1953-1960	94-96
Acadiane	1978-1987	92-93
Ami 6	1961-1969	97-101
Ami 8	1969-1979	102-104
Ami Super	1973-1976	104-105
Axel	1984-1988	146-147
Bijou	1959-1964	95-96
BX	1982-1994	124-133
BX 4 TC	1985-1986	131-132
C15	1984-2005	144-145
CX	1974-1991	48-61
CX estate: Series 1 and 2	1975-1991	58-60
CX saloon: Series 1	1974-1985	50-56
CX saloon: Series 2	1985-1989	57-58
DS and ID	1955-1975	26-47
DS saloon	1955-1975	29-35
D Spécial and D Super	1970-1975	37
DS/ID estate	1958-1975	37-39
DS/ID convertible	1958-1973	40-41
ID saloon	1957-1969	35-37
UK-built cars	1955-1965	46-47
Dyane	1967-1983	85-88
FAF	1977-1981	93-94
GS	1970-1980	108-117
GS Birotor	1973-1975	117-119
GSA	1979-1986	120-123
LN and LNA	1976-1986	134-137
M35	1969-1971	106-107
Méhari	1968-1987	88-89
Méhari 4x4	1979-1983	90
SM	1970-1975	62-71
Traction Avant	1934-1957	9-25
7CV	1934-1941	11-13
11CV	1934-1957	14-19
15 Six	1938-1956	19-21
UK-built cars	1935-1955	24-25
Visa	1978-1988	137-144

www.ingramcontent.com/pod-product-compliance
Lightning Source LLC
Chambersburg PA
CBHW040902250426
43672CB00034B/2985